EYEWITNESS TRAVEL TOP 10

BARCELONA

ANNELISE SORENSEN
RYAN CHANDLER

Left **Interior, Casa Lleó Morera** Right **La Rambla**

LONDON, NEW YORK,
MELBOURNE, MUNICH AND DELHI
www.dk.com

Produced by Departure Lounge, London

Reproduced by Colourscan, Singapore
Printed and bound in China by Leo
Paper Group

First published in Great Britain in 2002
by Dorling Kindersley Limited
80 Strand, London WC2R 0RL
A Penguin Company

**Copyright 2002, 2008 © Dorling
Kindersley Limited, London
Reprinted with revisions
2004, 2005, 2006, 2007, 2008**

A CIP catalogue record is available from
the British Library.

ISBN 978 1 40532 779 4

Within each Top 10 list in this book, no
hierarchy of quality or popularity is
implied. All 10 are, in the editor's
opinion, of roughly equal merit.

Contents

Barcelona's Top 10

Left **Jardins Mossèn Jacint Verdaguer** Centre **Bar, Pachito** Right **Terrace café, Barri Gòtic**

Left **Plaça de Sant Felip Neri, Barri Gòtic** Right **Stained-glass ceiling, Palau de la Música catalana**

Key to abbreviations
Adm admission charge payable **DA** disabled access

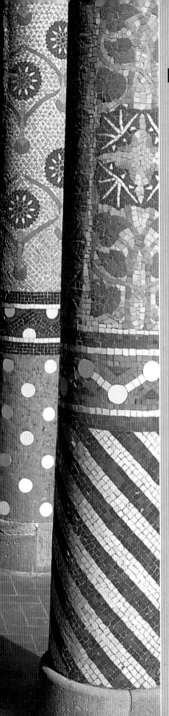

BARCELONA'S
TOP 10

BARCELONA'S TOP 10

🔟 Barcelona's Highlights

With warm, crystal-clear waters lapping its sandy shores and mountains nuzzling up to its northern edge, this glittering jewel in the Mediterranean is blessed with desirable geographical genes. From the buoyant, revamped port area to the atmospheric medieval streets of the Barri Gòtic and the beautiful Modernista *buildings of the Eixample, Barcelona has it all. A host of treasure-filled museums, architectural wonders, lively beaches and enchanting squares provide the icing on the cake.*

Sagrada Família
The enduring symbol of the city and its *Modernista* legacy is this church, Gaudí's other-worldly *pièce de résistance*. Piercing the Barcelona skyline are eight of the twelve planned spires *(above)* that have so far been built. See pp8–10.

La Rambla
Barcelona's centrepiece, this 1-km- (0.6-mile) long, thriving pedestrian thoroughfare *(above)* cuts a wide swathe through the old town, from Plaça de Catalunya to the glistening Mediterranean. See pp12–13.

Barcelona Cathedral
Dominating the heart of the old town is this magnificent Gothic Cathedral *(above)*, with a soaring, elaborate façade and a graceful, sun-dappled cloister containing palm trees and white geese. See pp14–15.

Parc de la Ciutadella
A verdant oasis in the city centre, Barcelona's largest park is crisscrossed with pleasant paths. It boasts a zoo, two museums, and a lavish *Modernista* fountain *(right)*. See pp16–17.

⑤ Museu Nacional d'Art de Catalunya

The stately Palau Nacional *(right)* is home to the Museu Nacional d'Art de Catalunya (MNAC), which holds one of the most extensive collections of Romanesque art in the world. The works were rescued from churches around Catalonia in the 1920s. *See pp18–19.*

⑥ La Pedrera

Unmistakably Gaudí, this *Modernista* marvel *(below)* seems to grow from the very pavement itself. Fluid and eerily alive, its curving façade sprouts writhing wrought-iron balconies. A cluster of mosaic chimneys keeps watch over the rooftop like shrewd-eyed knights. *See pp20–21.*

⑦ Fundació Joan Miró

An incomparable blend of art and architecture, this spacious museum, awash with natural light, showcases the work of Joan Miró, one of Catalonia's greatest 20th-century artists. Paintings, sculptures, drawings and textiles represent 60 prolific years. *See pp22–3.*

⑧ Museu Picasso

Housed in a medieval palace complex, this museum charts Picasso's rise to fame with an extensive collection of his early works, including numerous masterful portraits painted at the age of 13. *See pp24–5.*

⑨ Palau de la Música Catalana

No mere concert hall, the aptly named Palace of Catalan Music *(left)* is one of the finest, and most exemplary, *Modernista* buildings in Barcelona. *See pp26–7.*

⑩ Museu d'Art Contemporani & Centre de Cultura Contemporània

The city's gleaming contemporary art museum *(above)* and it's cutting-edge cultural centre have sparked an urban revival in the El Raval area. *See pp28–9.*

TOP 10 Sagrada Família

Nothing quite prepares you for the impact of the Sagrada Família up close. A fantastical tour de force of the imagination, Antoni Gaudí's ambitious church has provoked endless controversy. After a lifetime of dedication, the church was only partially complete when Gaudí died in 1926 and, as a work in progress, it offers the unique chance to watch the eighth wonder of the world in the making. During the last 80 years and at incalculable cost, sculptors and architects have added their own touches to Gaudí's dream. Now financed by over a million visitors each year, it is estimated the project will be complete by 2030.

Passion Façade

🔍 Try sitting in a terrace bar on nearby Avinguda Gaudí and drinking in the view of Gaudí's masterpiece illuminated at night.

🎯 For the best photos, get to the temple before 8am: the light on the Nativity Façade is excellent and the tour buses haven't yet arrived.

Look out for the cryptogram on the Passion Façade, where all the numbers add up to the age of Christ at the time of his death.

• Entrances: C/Marina & C/Sardenya • Map G2
• 93 207 30 31
• www.sagradafamilia.org
• Metro: Sagrada Família.
• Open: Oct–Mar: 9am–6pm daily; Apr–Sep: 9am–8pm daily
• Adm: €8 • Guided tours: May–Oct: 11am, 1pm, 3pm & 5pm daily; Nov–Apr: 11am & 1pm daily • €3.50
• Limited DA

Top 10 Features

1. Nativity Façade
2. Passion Façade
3. Spiral Staircases
4. Spires
5. Hanging Model
6. Nave
7. Rosedoor Cloister
8. Crypt Museum
9. Apse
10. Unfinished Business

Nativity Façade
Gaudí's love of nature is visible in this façade *(above)*. Up to a hundred plant and animal species are sculpted into the stone, and the two main columns are supported by turtles.

Passion Façade
Started in 1978 and completed in 2002, this façade by Josep Subirachs represents the pain and sacrifice of Jesus. The difference between the Gothic feel of Subirachs' style and the intricacy of Gaudí's original work has not been without polemic.

Spiral Staircases
These helicoidal stone stairways, which wind up the bell towers, look like snail shells. They allow access to the towers.

Spires
For a close-up look at the gargoyles and mosaic tiling on the spires *(left)*, scale the bell tower stairs – or ride up in a lift. The views are equally spectacular *(see p55)*. Not for sufferers of vertigo.

For more churches in Barcelona **See pp38–9**

Hanging Model
This bizarre contraption in the crypt museum is testimony to Gaudí's ingenuity. Gaudí created this 3D construction – made of chains and small weighted sacks of sand – as a model for the arches and vaulted ceilings of the Colonia Güell crypt. No-one, in the history of architecture, had ever designed a building like this.

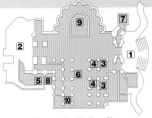

Sagrada Familia Floor Plan

Nave
The immense central body of the temple, still in progress, is made up of leaning, tree-like columns with branches spreading out across the ceiling. Inspired by towering redwood trees, the overall effect is that of a stone forest.

Rosedoor Cloister
In the only cloister to be finished by Gaudí, the imagery is surprisingly modern. Thought to be inspired by the anarchist riots that began in 1909 (see pp30–31), the devil's temptation of man is represented by the sculpture of a serpent wound around a bomb-throwing rebel.

Crypt Museum
Gaudí now lies in the crypt (left) and his tomb is visible from the museum. Recently renovated to include a small cinema, the museum offers information about the temple's construction. The highlight is the maquette workshop, producing scale plaster and stone models for the ongoing work.

Apse
Adorned with lizards, serpents and two gigantic snails, the apse was the first section of the temple to be completed by Gaudí.

Unfinished Business
The church buzzes with activity: sculptors dangle from spires; stone masons carve huge slabs of stone; and cranes and scaffolding litter the site. Observing the construction in progress (left) enables visitors to grasp the monumental scale of the project.

Sight Guide
The entrances to the Sagrada Familia are on C/Sardenya (along with the gift shop and one of the bell tower lifts) and C/Marina. On the C/Marina side, there are stairs (and another lift) to the other bell towers, and stairs to the museum below. If you don't want to pay the charge to use the lifts (€2), be warned – it's quite a climb.

Left **Spiral staircase** Right **Detail of doorway, Passion Façade**

🔟 Key Sagrada Família Dates

1882
The first stone of the Sagrada Família is officially laid, with architect Francesc del Villar heading the project. Villar soon resigns after disagreements with the church's religious founders.

1883
The young, up-and-coming Antoni Gaudí is commissioned as the principal architect. He goes on to devote the next 40 years of his life to the project: by the end he even lives on the premises.

1889
The crypt is completed, ringed by a series of chapels, one of which is later to house the tomb of Gaudí.

1904
The final touches are made to the Nativity Façade, which depicts Jesus, Mary and Joseph amid a chorus of angels.

1925
The first of 18 bell towers, 100 m (328 ft) in height, is finished.

Stained-glass window

1926
On 10 June, Gaudí is killed by a tram while crossing the street near his beloved church. No-one recognizes the city's most famous architect.

1936
The advent of the Spanish Civil War brings construction of the Sagrada Família to a halt for some 20 years. During this time, Gaudí's studio and the crypt in the Sagrada Família are burned by revolutionaries, who despise the Catholic church for siding with the nationalists.

1987–1990
Artist Josep Maria Subirachs (b 1927) takes to living in the Sagrada Família just as his famous predecessor did. Subirachs completes the statuary of the Passion Façade. His angular, severe and striking sculptures draw both criticism and praise.

2000
On 31 December, the nave is at long last declared complete.

2010–2030
The whole nave and apse is projected to be fully roofed by 2010. The completion of the entire Sagrada Família is forecast for 2030, though this depends largely on funding. The building of the Sagrada Família – as Gaudí intended – relies on donations from the public. With so many paying visitors pouring in daily, construction work is gaining momentum.

For more on Modernista *architecture* **See pp32–3**

Antoni Gaudí

A flag bearer for the late 19th-century Modernista movement, Antoni Gaudí is Barcelona's most famous architect. A devout Catholic and a strong Catalan nationalist, he led an almost monastic existence, consumed by his architectural vision and living in virtual poverty for most of his life. In 2001, he was beatified and there are currently moves within the Catalan Catholic Church to declare him a saint.

Chimneypot, Casa Vicens

Gaudí's extraordinary legacy dominates the architectural map of Barcelona. His name itself comes from the Catalan verb *gaudir*, "to enjoy", and an enormous sense of exuberance and playfulness pervades his work. As was characteristic of Modernisme, nature prevails, not only in the decorative motifs, but also in the very structure of Gaudí's buildings. His highly innovative style is also characterized by intricate wrought-iron gates and balconies and *trencadís* tiling.

Antoni Gaudí (1852–1926)

Trencadís Tiling

Gaudí's revolutionary use of *trencadís* tiling, a decorative art form which consisted of smashing up ceramics and piecing them back together in mosaic patterns, is particularly prevalent at Parc Güell. Another fine example of this technique is the rooftop of La Pedrera where some of the chimneys were tiled using hundreds of broken *cava* bottles.

Trencadís-tiled lizard, Parc Güell

🔟 La Rambla

There may be no better place in the country to indulge in the Spanish ritual of the paseo (stroll) than on this wide, pedestrian street that is anything but pedestrian. An orgy of activity day and night, La Rambla is voyeuristic heaven. Spray-painted human statues stand motionless among the passing crowds; buskers croon crowd-pleasing classics; caricaturists deftly sketch faces; bustling stalls create an open-air market of bright bouquets and chattering parakeets; and round-the-clock kiosks sell everything from The Financial Times to porn videos.

Street performer

🔵 Kick back at the Cafè de l'Òpera at No. 74 *(see p42)* and soak up the Rambla ambience with a cool *granissat* (crushed ice drink) in hand.

⚫ Be warned: La Rambla is rife with pick-pockets.

• Map L2–L6
• Metro: Catalunya; Liceu; Drassanes.
• Gran Teatre del Liceu: open 10am–1pm daily; guided tour: 10am (€8.50); box office: 8:30am–8:30pm Mon–Sat • Mercat de La Boqueria: open 7am–8pm Mon–Sat • DA
• Palau de la Virreina: open 11am–2pm, 4–8:30pm Tue–Sat, 11am–3pm Sun; free • DA
• Centre d'Art Santa Mònica: open 11am–8pm Tue–Sat, 11am–3pm Sun; free
• Església de Betlem: open 8am–1:30pm & 5:30–8pm daily

Top 10 Attractions

1. Gran Teatre del Liceu
2. Monument a Colom
3. Mercat de La Boqueria
4. Flower & Bird Stalls
5. Font de Canaletes
6. Miró Mosaic
7. Palau de la Virreina
8. Centre d'Art Santa Mònica
9. Bruno Quadras Building
10. Església de Betlem

Gran Teatre del Liceu

The city's grand opera house *(above)*, founded in 1847, brought Catalan opera stars such as Montserrat Caballé to the world. Twice gutted by fire, it has been fully restored.

Monument a Colom

Pointing resolutely out to sea, this statue *(above right)* of Christopher Columbus (1888) commemorates his return to Spain after discovering the Americas. An elevator takes visitors to the top for sensational views *(see p54)*.

Mercat de La Boqueria

A cacophonous shrine to food, this cavernous market has it all, from stacks of fruit to suckling pigs and writhing lobsters.

For sights in the Barri Gòtic & La Ribera See pp70–73

Flower & Bird Stalls

Will the real Rambla please stand up? Amid the here-today-gone-tomorrow street performers and tourists, the true Rambla old-timers are the flower and bird stalls that flank the pedestrian walkway. Many of the stalls have been family-run for decades.

Font de Canaletes

Ensure your return to the city by drinking from this 19th-century fountain, inscribed with the legend that all who drink from it "will fall in love with Barcelona and always return".

La Rambla

Miró Mosaic

Splashed on the walkway on La Rambla is a colourful pavement mosaic *(above)* by Catalan artist Joan Miró. His signature abstract shapes and primary colours unfold at your feet.

Palau de la Virreina

Constructed by the viceroy of Peru in 1778 – the name means "Palace of the Viceroy's Wife" – this Neo-Classical palace hosts a range of temporary exhibitions, from sculpture to photography to video.

Centre d'Art Santa Mònica

Once the hallowed haunt of rosary beads and murmured prayers, this former 17th-century monastery was reborn in the 1980s. Thanks to a massive government-funded facelift, it is now a cutting-edge contemporary art centre. Temporary exhibitions run the gamut from large-scale video installations to sculpture and photography.

Bruno Quadras Building

Once an umbrella factory, this playful, late 19th-century building *(left)* is festooned with umbrellas.

Església de Betlem

A relic from a time when the Catholic Church was rolling in pesetas (and power), this hulking 17th-century church is a seminal reminder of when La Rambla was more religious than risqué.

For sights in El Raval See pp80–83

Barcelona's Top 10

✪10 Barcelona Cathedral

From its Gothic cloister and Baroque chapels to its splendid, 19th-century façade, the Cathedral, dating from 1298, is an amalgam of architectural styles, each one paying homage to a period in Spain's religious history. Records show that an early Christian baptistry was established here in the 6th century, later replaced by a Romanesque basilica in the 11th century, which gave way to the current Gothic Cathedral. This living monument still functions as the Barri Gòtic's spiritual hub.

Main entrance

🚇 Bask in the Cathedral's Gothic glory at the outdoor terrace of Estruch café on Plaça de la Seu.

🎵 Organ and choral concerts are usually held monthly; enquire at the Pia Almoina.

Watch *sardanes* – Catalonia's regional dance – in Plaça de la Seu (6pm Sat, noon Sun).

• Plaça de la Seu
• Map M3 • 93 315 15 54 • Metro: Liceu, Jaume I
• Cathedral: open 8am–7:30pm daily (8pm Sun); numerous services daily; €4; free access: 8am–12:45pm (1:45pm Sun) & 5:15–7:30pm
• Casa de L'Ardiaca: open Sep–Jul: 9am–8:45pm Mon–Fri, 9am–1pm Sat; Aug: 9am–7:30pm Mon–Fri; free
• Museu Diocesà: open 10am–2pm & 5–8pm Tue–Sat, 11am–2pm Sun; €6

Top 10 Features

1. Main Façade
2. Choir Stalls
3. Cloister
4. Crypt of Santa Eulàlia
5. Capella del Santíssim Sacrament i Crist de Lepant
6. Capella de Sant Benet
7. Capella de Santa Llúcia
8. Nave & Organ
9. Pia Almoina & Museu Diocesà
10. Casa de L'Ardiaca

Main Façade

The 19th-century façade *(right)* – reaching up to 70 m (230 ft) – draws your gaze up. Flanking the eye-catching entrance are twin towers, *Modernista* stained-glass windows and 100 carved angels.

Choir Stalls

The lavish choir stalls (1340), crowned with wooden spires, are decorated with colourful coats of arms *(left)* by artist Joan de Borgonya.

Cloister

Graced with a fountain, palm trees and roaming geese, the cloister dates back to the 14th century. The mossy fountain is presided over by a small, iron statue *(right)* of Sant Jordi (St George).

 For more churches in Barcelona See pp38–9

4 Crypt of Santa Eulàlia

In the crypt's centre lies the graceful alabaster sarcophagus (1327) of Santa Eulàlia, Barcelona's first patron saint. Reliefs depict her martyrdom.

5 Capella del Santíssim Sacrament i Crist de Lepant

This 15th-century *capella* (chapel) features the Christ de Lepanto, which, legend has it, guided the Christian fleet in its 16th-century battle against the Ottoman Turks.

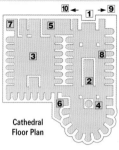

Cathedral Floor Plan

6 Capella de Sant Benet

Honouring Sant Benet, the patron saint of Europe, this chapel showcases the 15th-century altarpiece *Transfiguration of the Lord (below)* by illustrious Catalan artist Bernat Martorell.

7 Capella de Santa Llúcia

This lovely Romanesque chapel is dedicated to Santa Llúcia, the saint of sight and vision. On her saint's day (13 December), the blind (*els cecs*) arrive in droves to pray at her chapel.

8 Nave & Organ

The immense nave *(below)* is supported by soaring Gothic buttresses, which arch over 16 chapels. The 16th-century organ looming over the interior fills the Cathedral with music during services.

Cathedral Guide

The most impressive entrance to the Cathedral is its main portal on Plaça de la Seu. As you enter, to the left lie a series of chapels, the organ and elevators that take you to the terrace for phenomenal views of the Barri Gòtic (*see p55*). The Casa de L'Ardiaca lies to the right of the Cathedral's main entrance (at Carrer Santa Llúcia 1); the Museu Diocesà is to the left (at Avinguda de la Catedral 4).

9 Pia Almoina & Museu Diocesà

The 11th-century Pia Almoina, once a rest house for pilgrims and the poor, houses the Museu Diocesà, with Romanesque and Gothic works of art from around Catalonia.

10 Casa de L'Ardiaca

Originally built in the 12th century, the Archdeacon's House sits near what was once the Bishop's Gate in the city's Roman walls. Expanded over the centuries, it now includes a leafy patio with a fountain.

 For more sights in the Barri Gòtic & La Ribera See pp70–73

15

Parc de la Ciutadella

Unfolding languidly just to the east of the old town, this green, tranquil oasis provides a welcome respite from the city centre. Built in the late 1860s on the site of a former military fortress (ciutadella), the park was artfully designed to offer Barcelona's citizens an experience of nature (shady corners, paths and greenhouses), recreation (rowing boats on the lake) and culture (two museums). The 1888 Universal Exhibition was held here and in preparation the city's great Modernista architects were brought in to work their magic. Lluís Domènech i Montaner created the eye-catching Castell dels Tres Dragons (today the Zoological Museum) and a young Antoni Gaudí helped design the flamboyant Cascade Fountain.

Statuary on the Cascade Fountain

⊙ Pick up a picnic at the bustling Santa Caterina food market (northwest of the park), or have a drink and a snack within the colonial elegance of the Hivernacle café. If it's a hot day, cool down with a bowl of *gazpacho*.

• Main entrance: Pg Pujades • Map R4
• Park: open 8am–10:30pm daily; free; DA
• Zoo: open Nov–Feb: 10am–5pm daily; Mar–May & Oct: 10am–6pm daily; Jun–Sep: 10am–7pm daily; €15, children €9; DA
• Museu de Zoologia & Museu de Geologia: open 10am–6:30pm Tue–Sat, 10am–2:30pm Sun; €3.50 joint ticket; DA

Top 10 Sights

1. Cascade Fountain
2. Arc de Triomf
3. Parc Zoològic
4. Llac
5. Antic Mercat del Born
6. Museu de Zoologia
7. Museu de Geologia
8. Hivernacle & Umbracle
9. Parlament de Catalunya
10. Homenatge a Picasso

Cascade Fountain
One glimpse of this fanciful, Baroque-style fountain *(right)* and you'll probably guess Gaudí had a hand in its creation. Winged horses with serpent tails rear over a mossy waterfall and chubby cherubs giggle at play amid jets of water.

Arc de Triomf
The grandest entrance to the park is the Arc de Triomf *(above)*, designed for the 1888 Exhibition by Josep Vilaseca i Casanoves. Topping the arch are angels tooting horns and offering wreaths.

Parc Zoològic
These colourful flamingos are just some of the stars at this child-friendly zoo, which also has pony rides, electric cars and a train *(see p62)*.

Llac
In the centre of the park is a placid, man-made lake *(above),* where you can rent a boat for half an hour or more.

Antic Mercat del Born
The outline of Barcelona's medieval streets, houses, shops and palaces are revealed below this old market. The foundations date from 1714, the year Felipe V and his French allies entered the city.

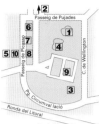

Park Plan

Museu de Zoologia
The Zoological Museum is housed in Domènech i Montaner's striking building. The centrepiece is a collosal whale skeleton, which hangs amid scores of stuffed animals, including a sabre-toothed tiger.

Museu de Geologia
Roam to your heart's content among 15,000 minerals, 14,000 rocks and over 100,000 palaeontological pieces, including a collection of Catalonian fossils.

Parlament de Catalunya
Housed in the lovely Palau de la Ciutadella *(below),* 1891, is the Catalonian Parliament, where Pascual Maragall (the President of Catalonia) and other political groups meet. In front is the Plaça d'Armes and a graceful water-lily pond with a sculpture (1907) by Josep Llimona.

Homenatge a Picasso
Antoni Tàpies toasts Picasso's cubist legacy with an abstract creation of his own. Tàpies' *Homage to Picasso* – a large glass cube filled with furnishings and abstract objects – requires some mental gymnastics to decipher its meaning.

Hivernacle & Umbracle
Palm trees and other tropical vegetation exude humidity inside the late 19th-century Hivernacle and Umbracle greenhouses *(above).* The latter was designed by architect Josep Fontseré, the former by Josep Amargós.

Park Guide
Two metro stops provide access to the park: to approach through the grand Arc de Triomf, disembark at the metro station of the same name. If you're heading to the zoo, get off at Barceloneta metro stop, which is within easy walking distance.

For more of Barcelona's parks See pp56–7

Museu Nacional d'Art de Catalunya

Incorporating one of the most important medieval art collections in the world, the Museu Nacional d'Art de Catalunya (MNAC) is housed in the majestic Palau Nacional, built in 1929. The high point of the museum is the Romanesque art section, consisting of the painted interiors of churches from the Pyrenees dating from the 11th and 12th centuries. There is also the Thyssen-Bornemisza Collection, with works from the Gothic period to the Rococo; the Cambó Bequest, with works by the likes of Goya and Zurbarán; and a collection of works by Catalan artists from the early 19th century to the 1940s.

Palau Nacional façade

⬤ On the first floor there is a top-notch restaurant in impressively elegant surroundings. There's also a great café in the Oval Room.

⬤ There are spectacular city views from the entrance to the huge glass foyer.

• Palau Nacional, Parc de Montjuïc
• Map B4
• Metro: Espanya
• 93 622 03 76
• www.mnac.es
• Open 10am–7pm Tue–Sat, 10am–2:30pm Sun
• Adm: €8.50; con €6 (valid for one month); free first Sun of the month • Guided tours by appointment • DA

Top 10 Exhibits

1. Interior: Sant Joan de Boí
2. Frescoes: Sant Climent de Taüll
3. Virgin: Ger
4. Crucifix of Batlló Majesty
5. Murals: Santa Maria de Taüll
6. Apse: Santa Maria d'Aneu
7. Madonna of Humility
8. The Madonna of the Councillors
9. Retaule de Sant Agustí
10. Cambó Bequest

Interior: Sant Joan de Boí

Painted in French Romanesque style, this is one of the museum's most complete church interiors (c.1100). The boldly kinetic *Stoning of St Stephen* is set beside a dramatic depiction of heaven and hell. Other scenes depict saints in heaven, animals and minstels.

[Floor plan labels: Toilets, Café, Book, Gift shop]

Frescoes: Sant Climent de Taüll

Among the most important examples of European Romanesque is the Taüll interior *(left)*, a melange of Byzantine, French and Italian influences. The apse is dominated by *Christ in Majesty* and the symbols of the four Evangelists and the Virgin, with the apostles beneath.

For more sights in Montjuïc **See pp88–91**

Virgin: Ger
This outstanding 12th-century sculpture (*left*) came from a series that evolved in Catalonia and the Pyrenees. Mary sits rigid in flowing robes, acting as a human throne for the young Christ, who raises his hand in blessing.

Crucifix of Batlló Majesty
This splendid, mid-12th-century wooden carving (*left*) depicts Christ on the cross with open eyes and no signs of suffring, because he has defeated death. He is clothed in royal robes.

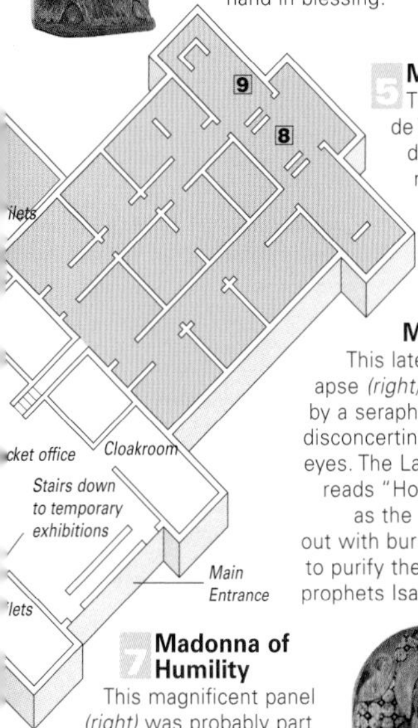

Murals: Santa Maria de Taüll
The well-preserved interior of Santa Maria de Taüll (c.1123) gives an idea of how incredibly colourful the Romanesque churches must have been. The symbolism concentrates on Jesus's early life, with scenes of the Wise Men and John the Baptist.

Apse: Santa Maria d'Aneu
This late 11th-century apse (*right*) is dominated by a seraph, its six wings disconcertingly covered in eyes. The Latin inscription reads "Holy, holy, holy" as the angel reaches out with burning hot coals to purify the words of the prophets Isaiah and Elijah.

Madonna of Humility
This magnificent panel (*right*) was probably part of a triptych. The Virgin, with the Child on her lap, sits on a throne surrounded by angels.

The Madonna of the Councillors
Commissioned by Barcelona's city council in 1443, this work by Lluís Dalmau is rich in political symbolism. It reveals the head councillors, supported by saints and martyrs, kneeling before a regally enthroned Virgin.

Retaule de Sant Agustí
This altarpiece (1463–85), by master painter Jaume Huguet, is a dramatic illustration of the wealth of the medieval Church.

Cambó Bequest
A collection of mostly Renaissance and Baroque art, donated by Francesc Cambó. Work by Flemish artists such as Rubens reveal the transformation from Gothic to Rennaissance, while the darker visions of Goya and Zurbarán represent Spain's 18th-century Golden Age.

Key
- Romanesque Art Gallery
- Sala Oval
- Gothic Art Gallery
- Renaissance and Baroque Art
- Thyssen-Bornemisza Collection

Gallery Guide
The Romanesque and Gothic galleries, the Cambó Bequest and the Thyssen-Bornemisza Collection are located on the main floor. On the lower level there are temporary exhibits.

Map labels: ﬁlets · cket office · Cloakroom · Stairs down to temporary exhibitions · Main Entrance · ﬁlets

For information on the Font Màgica, located at the bottom of the steps that lead up to the Palau Nacional, **See p89**

🔟 La Pedrera

Completed in 1910, this fantastic, undulating apartment block, with its out-of-this-world roof and delicate wrought ironwork, is one of the most emblematic of all Gaudí's works. La Pedrera (the Stone Quarry), also known as Casa Milà, was Gaudí's last great civic work before he dedicated the rest of his life to the Sagrada Família (see pp8–10). Restored to its former glory in 1996 after years of decay, La Pedrera now contains a museum dedicated to the architect, the exhibition centre of the Caixa de Catalunya, a furnished museum apartment, as well as private residences. What makes La Pedrera so magical is that every last detail, from door knobs to light fittings, bears the hallmark of Gaudí's visionary genius.

Façade, La Pedrera

🍷 During the summer months, a terrace bar on the roof (9pm–midnight Fri & Sat) allows visitors to enjoy a drink and live music amid the spectacular surroundings. Reservations essential *(see p47)*.

🕗 For more information on temporary exhibitions held here, check the website of the Caixa de Catalunya (http://obrasocial. caixacatalunya.es)

• *Passeig de Gracia 92*
• *Map E2*
• *90 240 09 73*
• *Metro: Diagonal*
• *Open: 10am–8pm daily (Nov–Feb: 9am–6:30pm; mid-Jun–late Jul: 9am–midnight Fri & Sat with reservation – 90 210 12 12)*
• *Adm: €8; con €4.50 (Free admission to the temporary exhibition space.)*

Top 10 Features

1. Façade & Balconies
2. Roof
3. Espai Gaudí
4. El Pis de la Pedrera
5. Interior Courtyard: C/Provença
6. Gates
7. Temporary Exhibition Room
8. Interior Courtyard: Pg de Gràcia
9. Auditorium
10. La Pedrera Shop

Façade & Balconies

Defying the laws of gravity, La Pedrera's irreverent curved walls are held in place by undulating horizontal beams attached to invisible girders. Intricate wrought-iron balconies *(above)* are a perfect example of the artisan skill so integral to *Modernisme*.

Espai Gaudí

A series of drawings, photos, maquettes and multimedia displays helps visitors grasp Gaudí's architectural wizardry. The museum is housed in the breathtaking, vaulted attic with its 270 brick arches forming skeletal corridors.

Roof

The strikingly surreal rooftop sculpture park *(above)* has chimneys resembling medieval warriors and huge ventilator ducts twisted into bizarre organic forms *(below)*; not to mention good views over the Eixample.

  For more on Modernista *architecture* **See pp32–3**

El Pis de La Pedrera

This furnished *Modernista* flat *(right)*, set up with period furniture, reconstructs a typical bourgeois flat of late 19th-century Barcelona. It provides an engaging contrast between the staid middle-class conservatism of the era and the undeniable wackiness of the building itself.

Interior Courtyard: C/Provença

A brigade of guides take hordes of visitors through here each day. A closer inspection of this first courtyard reveals beautiful mosaics and wall paintings lining a swirling fairytale staircase.

Gates

The mastery involved in these huge, wrought-iron gates reveals the influence of Gaudí's predecessors – four generations of artisan metal-workers. The use of iron is integral to many of Gaudí's buildings.

Temporary Exhibition Room

This gallery space, run by the Caixa de Catalunya, holds regular free art exhibitions. It has shown work by Marc Chagall, Salvador Dalí, Francis Bacon and others. The ceiling *(above)* looks as if it has been coated with whisked egg whites.

Interior Courtyard: Pg de Gràcia

Like the first courtyard, here, too, is a grand, ornate staircase (left). This one is adorned with a stunning, floral ceiling painting.

Auditorium

The basement auditorium (currently closed for renovation) hosts regular conferences and concerts. The adjacent garden offers a glimpse of greenery.

Sight Guide

The Espai Gaudí (attic), El Pis (fourth floor) and the rooftop are all accessible by lift. The Temporary Exhibition Room is located up the staircase from the Pg de Gràcia courtyard. The courtyards, staircases and shops are also accessible from the main entrance on C/Provença.

La Pedrera Shop

A wide range of Gaudí-related memorabilia includes replicas of the warrior chimneys in ceramic and bronze.

For more on Antoni Gaudí **See p11**

Fundació Joan Miró

*This superb tribute to a man whose legacy as an artist and as a Catalan is
visible city-wide was founded in 1975 by Joan Miró himself, who wanted it to be
a contemporary arts centre. The museum holds more than 11,000 examples of
the artist's colourful paintings, sketches and sculptures. The 400 or so on display
trace Miró's development from an innovative Surrealist phase in the 1920s to
his place as one of the world's most challenging masters in the 1960s.*

Façade, Fundació Joan Miró

🍴 The elegant restaurant here is one of the best dining options in the area *(see p93)*.

🎵 In summer, live experimental music is showcased in the Fundació auditorium, usually on Thursday nights.

The gift shop has an original range of Miróesque curiosities, from tablecloths to champagne glasses, which make ideal presents.

• Av Miramar,
Parc de Montjuïc
• Map B4
• 93 443 94 70
• www.bcn.fjmiro.es
• Metro to Paral-lel,
then funicular; or metro
to Pl. Espanya, then bus
61; or buses 50 or 55
from the city centre
• Open: 10am–7pm Tue,
Wed, Fri & Sat (until
8pm Jul–Sep)
10am–9:30pm Thu,
10am–2:30pm Sun
• Adm: €7.50 (complete
collection); €4 (temp-
orary exhibitions) • DA

Top 10 Works of Art

1. *Tapis de la Fundaciò* (1979)
2. *L'Estel Matinal* (1940)
3. *Pagès Català al Cla de Lluna* (1968)
4. *Home i Dona Davant un Munt d'Excrement* (1935)
5. *Sèrie Barcelona* (1944)
6. *Font de Mercuri* (1937)
7. Sculpture Room
8. Terrace Garden
9. Visiting Exhibitions
10. Espai 13

Tapis de la Fundació

This immense, richly-coloured tapestry *(right)* represents the culmination of Miró's work with textiles, which began in the 1970s.

L'Estel Matinal

This is the only one of 23 paintings on paper known as the *Constellation Series* held by the Fundació. The *Morning Star's* introspective quality reflects Miró's state of mind at the outbreak of World War II, when he was living in hiding in Normandy. Spindly shapes of birds, women and heavenly bodies are suspended in front of an empty space.

Pagès Català al Cla de Lluna

The figurative painting *Catalan Peasant by Moonlight* *(left)* dates from the late 1960s and depicts two of Miró's favourite themes: earth and night. The figure of the peasant, a simple collage of colour, is barely decipherable, as the crescent moon merges with his sickle and the night sky takes on the rich green tones of earth.

For more on contemporary Catalan art, visit MACBA **See pp28–9**

4 Home i Dona Davant un Munt d'Excrement

Tortured, misshapened and lurid semi-abstract figures attempt to embrace against a black sky. Miró's pessimism at the time of *Man and Woman in Front of a Pile of Excrement (right)* would soon be confirmed by the outbreak of Spain's Civil War.

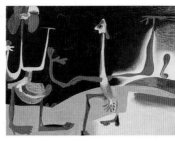

5 Sèrie Barcelona

The Fundació holds the only complete set of prints of this series of more than 50 black-and-white lithographs. This important collection is only occasionally on display.

6 Font de Mercuri

Alexander Calder donated the *Mercury Fountain* to the Fundació as a mark of his friendship with Miró. The work was an anti-fascist tribute, conceived in memory of the attack on the town of Almadén.

7 Sculpture Room

This room *(above)* focuses on Miró's sculptures from the mid-1940s to the late-1950s when he experimented first with ceramic, then bronze and finally with painted media and found objects. Outstanding works include *Sun Bird* (1946–9) and *Moon Bird* (1946–9).

8 Terrace Garden

More of Miró's vibrantly colourful and playful sculptures are randomly scattered on a spacious terrace *(right)*, from which you can appreciate city views and the rationalist architecture of Josep Lluis Sert's geometric building. The 3-m (10-ft) tall *Caress of a Bird* (1967) dominates the terrace.

9 Espai 13

This space showcases the experimental work of new artists from around the world. The exhibitions, which are based on a single theme each year, are usually radical and often make full use of new technologies.

9 Visiting Exhibitions

Over the years, these temporary exhibitions (usually held in the west wing) have included retrospectives of high-profile artists such as Rothko, Warhol and Magritte.

The New Gallery Extension

The Fundació celebrated its 25th anniversary in 2001 by opening a new extension (known as Sala K) to house 25 Miró paintings on long-term loan from a private collection.

The Fundació's collection is vast; only a portion of it is on show at any one time.

Museu Picasso

Pay homage to the 20th-century's most acclaimed artist at this treasure-filled museum. Highlighting Pablo Picasso's (1881–1973) formative years, the museum boasts the world's largest collection of the artist's early works. At the tender age of 10, Picasso was already revealing remarkable artistic tendencies. In 1895, aged 14, he and his family moved from the town of La Coruña to Barcelona, where Picasso blossomed as an artist. From precocious schoolbook sketches and powerful family portraits to selected works from his Blue and Rose periods, the Museu Picasso offers visitors the rare chance to discover the artist as he was discovering himself.

Entrance, Carrer Montcada

⊙ After you've had your fill of art, duck into the café *(see p42)* at the nearby Museu Textil, where you can enjoy a drink or light meal on a graceful outdoor patio.

⊙ The Museu Picasso is housed in a Gothic palace complex, replete with leafy courtyards, all of which can be explored.

• C/Montcada 15–23
• Map P4
• 93 256 30 21
• www.museu
picasso.bcn.cat
• Metro: Jaume I
• Open 10am–8pm
Tue–Sun • Adm: €6
(permanent collection);
€5 (temporary shows);
€8.50 (both collections);
free first Sun of month
(permanent collection
only) • DA

Top 10 Exhibits

1. *Hombre con boina* (1895)
2. *Autoretrato con peluca* (1896)
3. *Ciencia y Caridad* (1897)
4. Menu de Els Quatre Gats (1899–1900)
5. *Margot* & *La Nana* (1901)
6. *El Loco* (1904)
7. *Arlequín* (1917)
8. *Caballo corneado* (1917)
9. *Hombre sentado* (1917)
10. *Las Meninas* Series (1957)

Hombre con boina
This insightful portrait *(below)* reveals brush strokes – and a subject matter – that are far beyond a child who has just turned 13. No puppies or racing cars for the young Picasso; instead, he searched for the oldest men in the village and painted their portraits. The artist signed this portrait P Ruiz, because at this time he was still using his father's last name.

Autoretrato con peluca
At 14, Picasso painted a series of self-portraits, including *Self-portrait with Wig*, a whimsical depiction of how he might have looked during the time of his artistic hero, Velázquez.

Ciencia y Caridad
One of Picasso's first publicly exhibited paintings was *Science and Charity*. Picasso's father posed as the doctor.

For more museums See pp40–41

4 Menu de Els Quatre Gats

Picasso's premier Barcelona exhibition was in 1900, held at the Barri Gòtic café, Els Quatre Gats (see p45). The artist's first commission was the pen-and-ink drawing of himself and a group of artist friends in top hats, which graced the menu of this bohemian hang-out.

5 Margot & La Nana

Picasso's Margot (centre) is an evocative painting of a call-girl waiting for her next customer, while La Nana captures the defiant gaze and stance of a heavily rouged dwarf dancer.

6 El Loco

The Madman (left) is a fine example of Picasso's Blue period. This artistic phase, which lasted from 1901 to 1904, was characterized by melancholic themes and sombre colours.

7 Arlequín

A lifting of spirits led to Picasso's Neo-Classical period, typified by paintings like Arlequín, celebrating the light-hearted liberty of circus performers.

8 Caballo corneado

The anguished horse in this painting later appears in Guernica, which reveals the horrors of war. This work gives viewers the chance to observe the process that went into the creation of Picasso's most famous painting.

9 Hombre sentado

Works such as Man Sitting (right) confirmed Picasso's status as the greatest Analytic Cubist painter of the 20th century.

10 Las Meninas Series

Picasso's reverence for Velázquez culminated in this remarkable series of paintings (below), based on the Velázquez painting Las Meninas.

Gallery Guide

The museum is made up of five inter-connected medieval palaces. The permanent collection is arranged chronologically on the first and second floors of the first three palaces. Temporary exhibitions – usually showcasing one modern artist – are housed in the first and second floors of the last two palaces.

For more sights in the Barri Gòtic & La Ribera See pp70–73

🔟 Palau de la Música Catalana

Barcelona's Modernista movement reached its aesthetic culmination in this magnificent concert hall (1905–1908), designed by renowned architect Lluís Domènech i Montaner. The lavish façade, ringed by mosaic pillars and brick arches, just hints at what awaits within. Domènech's "garden of music" (as he called it) unfolds beyond the front doors, with each surface of the ornate foyer, from pillars to banisters, emblazoned with a flower motif. The concert hall – designed so that its height is the same as its breadth – is a celebration of natural light and forms, climaxing in a stained-glass, golden orb skylight that showers the hall with sunlight.

Façade, Palau de la Música Catalana

🍷 For a pre-concert, cocktail, settle in at the *Modernista* stained-glass bar just beyond the foyer.

🎵 Enjoy bargain early concerts, which usually happen twice monthly around 6 or 7pm on Saturday (Sep–Jun) and Sunday (Feb–May).

Buy tickets for the shows and guided tours from the ticket office round the corner at C/Sant Francesc de Paula 2: (90 244 28 82), open 10am–9pm daily.

- Sant Pere Mes Alt
- Map N2
- 90 244 28 82
- www.palaumusica.org
- Metro: Urquinaona
- guided tours every half hour: Sep–Jun 10am–3:30pm; Jul–Aug 10am–6pm (book a week in advance)
- Adm: €9 • Limited DA

Top 10 Features
1. Stained-Glass Ceiling
2. Stage
3. Stained-Glass Windows
4. Busts
5. Horse Sculptures
6. Chamber Music Room
7. Lluís Millet Hall
8. Foyer & Bar
9. Façade
10. Concert & Dance Series

Stained-Glass Ceiling
Topping the concert hall is a breathtaking, stained-glass inverted dome ceiling *(right)*, surrounded by 40 angels. By day, light streams through the fiery red and orange stained glass, illuminating the hall.

Stained-Glass Windows
Blurring the boundaries between the outdoors and the interior, Domènech encircled the concert hall with vast stained-glass windows to let in sunlight and reveal the changing times of day.

Stage
The main, semicircular stage *(above)* swarms with activity – even when no-one's performing. Eighteen mosaic and terracotta muses spring from the backdrop, playing everything from the harp to the castanets.

Busts
A bust of Catalan composer Josep Anselm Clavé (1824–74) celebrates the Palau's commitment to Catalan music. Facing him across the concert hall, a stern-faced, unruly-haired Beethoven *(above)* represents the hall's classical and international repertoire.

Horse Sculptures
Charging forth from the ceiling are winged horses (designed by architect Eusebi Arnau), infusing the concert hall with movement and verve. Also depicted is a representation of Wagner's chariot ride of the Valkyries, led by galloping horses that leap toward the stage.

Chamber Music Room
Designed as a rehearsal space, the semicircular, accoustically-sound Chamber Music Room is a smaller version of the massive concert hall one floor above. In its centre is an inlaid foundation stone commemorating the construction of the Palau.

Lluís Millet Hall
Named after Catalan composer Lluís Millet, this immaculately preserved lounge boasts gorgeous stained-glass windows. On the main balcony outside are rows of stunning mosaic pillars *(right)*.

Foyer & Bar
Modernista architects worked with ceramic, stone, wood, marble and glass, all of which Domènech used liberally, most notably in the opulent foyer and bar

Façade
The towering façade *(below)* reveals *Modernista* delights on every level. An elaborate mosaic represents the Orfeò Català choral society, founded in 1891.

Concert & Dance Series
Over 300 concerts and dance shows are staged each year, and seeing a show here is an experience not to be missed. For traditional Catalan dance and choral singing, look out for the *Cobla, Cor, i Dansa* series (usually begins February).

Orfeó Catalá
Perhaps the most famous choral group to perform here is the Orfeó Catalá, for whom the concert hall was originally built. This 90-person chorus performs regularly and holds a concert on 26 December every year. Book in advance.

For more sights in the Barri Gòtic & La Ribera **See pp70–73**

Museu d'Art Contemporani & Centre de Cultura Contemporània

Barcelona's sleek contemporary art museum looms in bold contrast to the surrounding area. Together with the nearby Centre de Cultura Contemporània (CCCB), the Museu d'Art Contemporani (MACBA) has provided a focal point for modern Barcelona since its opening in 1995, and, has played an integral part in the rejuvenation of El Raval. MACBA's permanent collection includes a slew of big-name Spanish and international contemporary artists, while excellent temporary exhibits feature everything from painting to video installations. The CCCB serves as a crossroads of contemporary culture with cutting-edge art exhibits, lectures and film screenings.

Gallery space, MACBA

🍴 Snack at the nearby restaurant Plaça dels Àngels (on Pl dels Àngels), which offers budget-priced nouvelle/Catalan food to a hip crowd.

- MACBA
- Plaça dels Àngels
- Map K2
- Metro: Catalunya
- 93 412 08 10
- www.macba.es
- Open Oct–Jun: 11am–7:30pm Mon & Wed–Fri, 10am–8pm Sat, 10am–3pm Sun; Jul–Sep: 11am–8pm Mon, Wed, Fri, 11am–midnight Thu, 10am–8pm Sat, 10am–3pm Sun
- Adm: €7.50 (all floors); €6 (2 floors); €4 (1 floor) Thu–Tue; €3.50 (all floors) Wed • DA

- CCCB
- Montalegre 5
- Map K1
- Metro: Catalunya
- 93 306 41 00
- www.cccb.org
- Open: 11am–8pm Tue–Sun
- Adm: €4.40; free first Wed of month

Top 10 Features

1. Interior Corridors
2. Visiting Artist's Space
3. Revolving Permanent Collection
4. Façade
5. Puzzle Area
6. *A Sudden Awakening*
7. Thinking & Reading Spaces
8. El Patio de les Donnes/CCCB
9. Temporary Exhibitions/CCCB
10. Plaça Joan Coromines

Interior Corridors
Space and light are omnipresent in the walkways between floors. Look through the glass panels onto the Plaça dels Àngels for myriad images before you even enter the gallery spaces.

Visiting Artist's Space
The *raison d'etre* of MACBA is this flexible area showing the best in contemporary art. Past exhibitions have included Zush and acclaimed painter Dieter Roth.

Revolving Permanent Collection
The permanent collection comprises over 2000 – mostly European – modern artworks, 10 per cent of which are on show at any one time. All major contemporary artistic trends are represented. This work *(right)* by Eduardo Arranz Bravo is titled *Homea* (1974).

For more museums See pp40–41

Façade
American architect Richard Meier's stark, white, geometrical façade makes a startling impression against the backdrop of this dilapidated working-class neighbourhood. Hundreds of panes of glass reflect the skateboarders who gather here daily.

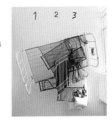

Puzzle Area
On the ground floor, several tables are set out with jigsaw puzzles *(left)*. The puzzles, which feature photos taken in neighbouring flats, give an intriguing glimpse of life in the nearby tenement buildings.

A Sudden Awakening
One of the only pieces of art on permanent display is Antoni Tàpies' deconstructed bed (1992–3), with its bedding flung across the wall in disarray *(above)*. Its presence to the right of the main entrance underlines Tàpies' importance as a key player in the world of Catalan modern art.

Thinking & Reading Spaces
Pleasant and unusual features of MACBA are the white leather sofas between the galleries. Usually next to a shelf of relevant books and a set of headphones, these spaces provide the perfect resting spot to contemplate – and learn more about – the art.

El Patio de les Donnes/CCCB
This courtyard *(left)* off Carrer Montalegre forms part of the neighbouring CCCB. An ultra-modern prismatic screen provides a mirror reflecting the 18th-century patio – a magical juxtaposition of different architectural styles.

Temporary Exhibitions/CCCB
Unlike MACBA, exhibitions at the CCCB tend to be more theme based than artist specific. Home to both a festival of cinema shorts (Sep) and the Sònar techno festival (Jun), the CCCB always manages to be at the forefront of the latest cultural trend.

Plaça Joan Coromines
The contrast between the modern MACBA, the new University building, the Tuscan-style CCCB and the 19th-century mock-Romanesque church make this square one of the most enchanting in the city. It is home to the terrace restaurants of MACBA and CCCB.

Sights Guide
The MACBA and CCCB have separate entrances, though they share the Plaça Joan Coromines courtyard. The CCCB is accessible from C/Montalegre and MACBA from the Plaça dels Àngels. Both multi-level galleries have flexible display spaces.

For more sights in El Raval **See pp80–83**

29

Left **La Setmana Tràgica, 1909** Right **Olympic Games, 1992**

🔟 Stages in Barcelona's History

1 BC: The Founding of a City
Barcino, as the city was first known, was founded in the 3rd century BC by Carthaginian Hamilcar Barca. It was taken by the Romans in 218 BC, but played second fiddle in the region to the provincial capital of Tarragona.

2 4th–11th Centuries: Early Invasions
As the Roman Empire began to fall apart in the 5th century, the Visigoths took over the city, followed by the Moors in the 8th century. Around AD 800, Charlemagne conquered the area with the help of the Pyrenean counts.

Poster, 1929 International Exhibition

3 12th–16th Centuries: The Middle Ages
During this period, Barcelona was the capital of a Catalan empire that included much of modern Spain and parts of the Mediterranean. The city's fortune was built on commerce, but as neighbouring Castile expanded into the New World, trading patterns shifted and the Catalan dynasty faltered. Barcelona fell into decline and came under Castilian domination.

4 1638–1652: Catalan Revolt
In reaction to the oppressive policies set out in Madrid, now ruled by the Austrian Habsburgs, various local factions, known as *Els Segadors*, revolted. Fighting began in 1640 and dragged on until 1652, when the Catalans and their French allies were defeated.

5 19th Century: Industry & Prosperity
Booming industry and trade with the Americas brought activity to the city. Immigrants poured in from the countryside, laying the foundations of prosperity but also the seeds of unrest. The old city walls came down, broad Eixample avenues were laid out and workers crowded the old city neighbourhoods left behind by the middle classes.

6 1888–1929: The Renaixença
This new wealth, showcased in the International Exhibitions of 1888 and 1929, sparked a Catalan renaissance. *Modernista* mansions sprouted up, and the nationalist bourgeoisie sparked a revival of Catalan culture, particularly of literature, theatre and art.

7 1909–1931: The Revolutionary Years
But discontent brewed among workers, Catalan nationalists, communists, Spanish fascists, royalists, anarchists and

republicans. In 1909, protests against the Moroccan war sparked a brutal riot, the *Setmana Tràgica* (Tragic Week). Lurching towards Civil War, Catalonia passed under a dictatorship before being declared a Republic in 1931.

8 1936–1975: Civil War & Franco

At the outbreak of war in 1936, Barcelona's workers and militants managed to fend off Franco's troops for a while. The city was taken by Fascist forces in 1939, prompting a wave of repression, particularly of the Catalan language which was banned in schools.

9 1975–1980s: Transition to Democracy

Franco's death in 1975 paved the way for democracy. The Catalan language was rehabilitated and, following the introduction of a new democratic constitution in Spain, Catalonia was granted regional autonomy. The first Catalan government was elected in 1980.

10 1992–Present Day: The Olympics & Beyond

Barcelona was catapulted onto the world stage in 1992 with the highly successful Olympics. Today, the city remains socialist in politics and ready to perceive itself as both Spanish and Catalan.

Civil War, 1936

Top 10 Historical Figures

1 Guifré the Hairy
The first Count of Barcelona (d. 897) is regarded as the founding father of Catalonia.

2 Ramon Berenguer IV
He united Catalonia and joined it with Aragon by marrying Princess Petronila in 1137.

3 Jaume I the Conqueror
This 13th-century warrior-king (d. 1276) conquered the Balearics and Valencia, laying the foundations for the empire.

4 Ramon Llull
Mallorcan philosopher and missionary, Llull (d. 1316) is the greatest figure in medieval Catalan literature.

5 Ferdinand the Catholic
King of Aragon and Catalonia (d.1516), he married Isabel of Castile, paving the way for the Kingdom of Spain's formation and the end of Catalan independence.

6 Idlefons Cerdà
19th-century urban planner who designed the Eixample.

7 Antoni Gaudí
An idiosyncratic and devout *Modernista* architect, Gaudí was responsible for Barcelona's most famous monuments.

8 Francesc Macià
This socialist nationalist politician proclaimed the birth of the Catalan Republic (1931) and Catalan autonomy (1932).

9 Lluís Companys
Catalan president during the Civil War. Exiled in France, he was arrested by the Gestapo in 1940 and returned to Franco, who had him executed.

10 Jordi Pujol
A centre-right regionalist politician, Pujol's Convergència i Unió coalition ruled Catalonia from 1980 to 2003.

Stained-glass windows, Casa Lleó Morera

Modernista Buildings

1 Sagrada Família
Dizzying spires and intricate sculptures adorn Gaudí's magical masterpiece. Construction began at the height of *Modernisme*, but is still in progress more than a century later. *See pp8–10.*

2 La Pedrera
This amazing apartment block, with its curving façade and bizarre rooftop, has all of Gaudí's architectural trademarks. Especially characteristic are the wrought-iron balconies and the ceramic mosaics decorating the entrance halls. *See pp20–21.*

3 Palau de la Música Catalana
Domènech i Montaner's magnificent concert hall is a joyous celebration of Catalan music. Ablaze with mosaic friezes, stained glass, ceramics and sculptures, it displays the full glory of

Chimneys and rooftop, Casa Batlló

the *Modernista* style. The work of Miquel Blay on the façade is rated as one of the best examples of *Modernista* sculpture in Barcelona. *See pp26–7.*

4 Hospital de la Santa Creu i de Sant Pau
In defiant contrast to the Eixample's symmetrical grid-like pattern, this ambitious project was planned around two avenues running at 45-degree angles to the Eixample streets. Started by Domènech i Montaner in 1905 and later completed by his son in 1930, the hospital pavilions are lavishly embellished with mosaics, stained glass and sculptures by Eusebi Arnau. The octagonal columns with floral capitals are inspired by those in the Monestir de Santes Creus *(see p124)*, to the south of Barcelona. *See p103.*

5 Fundacià Tàpies
With a rationally plain façade alleviated only by its *Mudéjar*-style brick work, this austere building, dating to 1886, was originally home to the publishing house Montaner i Simon. It bears the distinction of being the first *Modernista* work to be designed by Domènech i Montaner, which explains why it has so few of the ornate decorative touches that distinguish his later works. Home to the Fundacià Tàpies, it is now dominated by an enormous sculpture by the contemporary Catalan artist, Antoni Tàpies. *See p104.*

A ticket for La Ruta Modernista *includes discounted entry to three* Modernista *buildings and a map/guide* See p133

Casa Batlló

Illustrating Gaudí's nationalist sentiments, Casa Batlló, on La Mansana de la Discòrdia *(see p103)*, represents an allegory of the legend of Sant Jordi *(see p39)*. The roof is the dragon's back and the balconies, sculpted in the form of carnival masks, are the skulls of the dragon's victims. The polychrome façade reveals Gaudí's remarkable use of colour and texture. ◈ *Pg de Gràcia 43 • Map E2 • Open 9am–8pm daily • Adm €11 • DA*

Casa Amatller

The top of Casa Amatller's ochre-white façade bursts into a brilliant display of blue, cream and pink ceramics with burgundy florets. Architect Puig i Cadafalch's exaggerated decorative use of ceramics is typical of *Modernisme*. This Mansana de la Discòrdia *(see p103)* is a private house, but it is possible to access the ground and first floors, which house the Amatller Foundation. ◈ *Pg de Gràcia 41 • Map E2 • Open 10am–8pm Mon–Sat, 10am–3pm Sun • Free • DA*

Palau Güell

This palace is a fine example of Gaudí's experiments with structure, especially the use of parabolic arches to orchestrate space. Also remarkable is the use of unusual building materials, such as ebony and rare South American woods. *See p81.*

Casa de les Punxes (Casa Terrades)

Taking *Modernisme's* Gothic and medieval obsessions to extremes

that others seldom dared, Puig i Cadafalch created this imposing, castle-like structure between 1903 and 1905. Nicknamed the "House of Spines" because of its sharp, needle-like spires rising up from conical turrets, its true name is Casa Terrades. The flamboyant spires contrast with a façade that is, by *Modernista* standards, sparsely decorated. ◈ *Diagonal 416 • Map F2 • Closed to public*

Casa de les Punxes

Casa Lleó Morera

Ironwork, ceramics, sculpture and stained glass come together here in a synthesis of the decorative and fine arts. The interior of this house, by Domènech i Montaner, has some superb sculptures by Eusebi Arnau and some of the finest *Modernista* furniture in existence. ◈ *Pg de Gràcia 35 • Map E3 • Closed to public*

Left **Plaça de Catalunya** Right **Plaça Reial, Barri Gòtic**

10 Perfect Squares

Plaça Reial
The arcaded Plaça Reial, in the heart of the Barri Gòtic, is unique among Barcelona's squares, with its old-world charm, gritty urbanization and Neo-Classical flair. It is home to majestic, mid-19th-century buildings, Gaudí lampposts, a slew of happening bars and clubs, and an entertaining and colourful crowd of inner-city denizens. See p72.

Plaça de Catalunya
Barcelona's nerve centre is the huge Plaça de Catalunya, a lively hub from which all the city's activity seems to radiate. This square is most visitors first real glimpse of Barcelona. The airport bus stops here, as do RENFE trains and countless metro and bus lines. The square's commercial swagger is evident all around, headed by Spain's omnipresent department store, El Corte Inglés (see p139). Pigeons flutter chaotically in the square's centre, lively Peruvian

bands play to booming sound systems and hordes of travellers – from backpackers to tour groups – meander about. To add to the melting pot, the square is allegedly home to 25 people (mostly homeless immigrants). ❧ Map M1

Plaça del Rei
One of the city's best preserved medieval squares, the Barri Gòtic's Plaça del Rei is ringed by grand buildings. Among them is the 14th-century Palau Reial (see p71), which houses the Saló del Tinell, a spacious Catalan Gothic banqueting hall. ❧ Map N4

Plaça de Sant Jaume
Weighty with power and history, this is the administrative heart of modern-day Barcelona. The plaça is flanked by the city's two key government buildings, the stately Palau de la Generalitat and the 15th-century Ajuntament. See p71.

Café, Plaça Sant Josep Oriol, Barri Gòtic

Plaça de Rius i Taulet

The progressive, bohemian area of Gràcia, a former village annexed by Barcelona in 1897, still exudes a small-town ambience, where socializing with the neighbours means heading for the nearest *plaça*. Topping the list is this atmospheric square, with an impressive clock tower rising out of its centre. Bustling outdoor cafés draw buskers and a sociable crowd. ✆ *Map F1*

Façade, Plaça del Pi

Plaça de Sant Josep Oriol & Plaça del Pi

Old-world charm meets café culture in the Barri Gòtic's leafy Plaça de Sant Josep Oriol and Plaça del Pi, named after the pine trees (*pi*, in Catalan) that shade its nooks and crannies. The lovely Gothic church of Santa Maria del Pi *(see p38)* rises between the two squares. ✆ *Map M3 & M4*

Plaça Comercial

The buzzy Passeig del Born culminates in Plaça Comercial, an inviting square dotted with cafés and bars. It faces the 19th-century Born Market *(see p72)*, which will re-open in 2008 as a cultural centre and exhibition space. ✆ *Map P4*

Plaça del Sol

Tucked within the cosy grid of Gràcia, this square is surrounded by handsome 19th-century buildings. As evening descends, it becomes one of the most lively spots to start your night-time festivities, along with all the *Barcelonins* who mingle on the outdoor terraces. ✆ *Map F1*

Plaça de Santa Maria

The magnificent Església de Santa Maria del Mar *(see p76)* imbues its namesake *plaça*, in the El Born district, with a certain spiritual calm. Bask in its Gothic ambience, people watch, and soak up the sun at one of the outdoor terrace cafés. ✆ *Map N5*

Plaça de la Vila de Madrid

Mere steps from La Rambla *(see pp12–13)* is this spacious *plaça*, graced with the remains of a Roman necropolis. A remnant of Roman Barcino, the square sat just beyond the boundaries of the walled Roman city. A row of unadorned 2nd–4th-century AD tombs were discovered here in 1957. The complete remains are open to the public. ✆ *Map M2*

Left **Església del Betlem** Right **Temple Expiatori del Sagrat Cor**

🔟 Charming Churches & Chapels

Barcelona Cathedral

Barcelona's magnificent Gothic cathedral boasts an eye-catching façade and a peaceful cloister. *See pp14–15.*

Església de Santa Maria del Mar

The elegant church of Santa Maria del Mar (1329–83) is one of the finest examples of Catalan Gothic, a style characterized by measured simplicity. A spectacular stained-glass rose window illuminates the lofty interior. *See p76.*

Capella de Sant Miquel & Església al Monestir de Pedralbes

Inside the tranquil Monestir de Pedralbes *(see p111)* is a splendid Gothic cloister and the Capella de Sant Miquel, decorated with impressive murals by Catalan artist Ferrer Bassa in 1346. The adjoining graceful Gothic church contains the alabaster tomb of Queen Elisenda, the monastery's founder. ❧ *C/Baixada del Monestir 14 • Map A1 • Open 10am–2pm (church also open 7–8:30pm) Tue–Sun*

Santa Eulàlia, Barcelona Cathedral

Església de Sant Pau del Camp

Founded as a Benedictine monastery in the 9th century by Guifre II, a count of Barcelona, this church was rebuilt the following century. Its sculpted façade and intimate cloister with rounded arches bear all the trademarks of the Romanesque style. *See p83.*

Església de Sant Pere de les Puelles

Built in 801 as a chapel for troops stationed in Barcelona, this *església* later became a spiritual retreat for young noblewomen. The church was rebuilt in the 1100s and is notable today for its Romanesque central cupola and a series of capitals topped with carved leaves. Look out for two stone tablets depicting a Greek cross, which are from the original chapel. ❧ *Pl de Sant Pere • Map P2 • Open 8:45am–1pm, 5–7:30pm Mon–Fri; 8:45am–1pm, 4:30– 6:30pm Sat; 10am–2pm Sun*

Església de Santa Maria del Pi

This lovely Gothic church with its ornate stained-glass windows graces Plaça del Pi *(see p37)* with its elegant presence. ❧ *Pl del Pi • Map L3 • Open 9am–1:30pm & 4:30–9pm daily • DA*

Capella de Santa Àgata

Within the grand walls of the Palau Reial *(see p71)* is the lovely medieval Capella de Santa Àgata, with its striking stained-glass windows and a superb 15th-century altarpiece. ❧ *Pl del Rei • Map N3 • Open 10am–8pm Tue–Sat, 10am–3pm Sun (Oct–May: closed 2–4pm) • Adm*

Temple Expiatori del Sagrat Cor

Mount Tibidabo is an appropriate perch for this huge, over-the-top Neo-Gothic church, topped with a gold Christ with outstretched arms. The name Tibidabo takes its meaning from the words, "I shall give you" (*tibi dabo*), uttered by the Devil in his temptation of Christ. Zealously serving the devoted, the priest here performs the Eucharist throughout the day. ◈ *Tibidabo • Map B1 • Open 10:30am–7:30pm daily*

Capella de Sant Jordi

Inside the Palau de la Generalitat *(see p71)* is this fine 15th-century chapel, dedicated to Catalonia's patron saint. ◈ *Pl Sant Jaume • Map M4 • Guided tours 10:30am–1:30pm 2nd & 4th Sun of month*

Església de Betlem

La Rambla was once dotted with religious buildings, most built in the 17th and 18th centuries when the Catholic Church was flush with money. This *església* remains one of the most important functioning churches from this period. ◈ *C/ Xuclà 2 • Map L3 • Open 8am–1:30pm & 5:30–8pm daily • DA*

Gothic nave, Capella de Santa Àgata

Top 10 Catalan Saints & Virgins

1 Sant Jordi
Catalonia's patron saint is Saint George, whose dragon-slaying prowess is depicted all over the city.

2 Virgin Mercè
She became the female patron saint ob Barcelona in 1637. The most raucous festival in town is the Festes de La Mercè *(see p64)*.

3 Virgin of Montserrat
Catalonia's famous "Black Virgin" is the city's patron virgin.

4 Santa Eulàlia
Santa Eulàlia, Barcelona's first female patron saint, was martyred by the Romans when they took the city.

5 Santa Elena
Legend has it that Saint Helena converted to Christianity after discovering Christ's cross in Jerusalem in 346 AD.

6 Santa Llúcia
The saint of eyes and vision is celebrated on 13 December, when the blind come to worship at the Santa Llúcia chapel in the cathedral *(see pp14–15)*.

7 Sant Cristòfol
Though officially stripped of his sainthood as there was little evidence he existed, Saint Christopher was once the patron saint of travellers.

8 Sant Antoni de Padua
On 13 June, those seeking a husband or wife pray to the patron saint of love.

9 Santa Rita
Deliverer of the impossible, Santa Rita is prayed to by those searching for miracles.

10 Sant Joan
The night of Saint John *(see p64)* is celebrated with giant bonfires and fireworks.

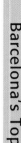
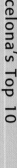

Left **Frank Gehry's** *Peix* *Right* **Camp Nou Stadium**

Museums

Museu Nacional d'Art de Catalunya

Discover Catalonia's rich Romanesque and Gothic heritage at this impressive museum, housed in the 1929 Palau Nacional. Striking medieval frescoes – many culled from ancient Pyrenean churches – are the highlight. *See pp18–19.*

Fundació Joan Miró

The airy, high-ceilinged galleries of this splendid museum are a fitting resting place for the bold, abstract works of Joan Miró, one of Catalonia's most acclaimed 20th-century artists. *See pp22–3.*

Museu Picasso

Witness the budding – and meteoric rise – of Picasso's artistic genius at this unique museum. One of the world's largest collections of the painter's early works. *See pp24–5.*

Museu d'Art Contemporani & Centre de Cultura Contemporània

Inaugurated in 1995, MACBA is Barcelona's centre for modern art. Combined with the neighbouring CCCB, the two buildings form an artistic and cultural hub in the heart of El Raval. Both regularly host temporary exhibitions: the MACBA showcases contemporary artists; the CCCB is more theme-based. *See pp28–9.*

Fundació Tàpies

Works by Catalan artist Antoni Tàpies are showcased in this graceful *Modernista* building. Venture inside to discover Tàpies' rich repertoire, from early collage works to large, abstract paintings, many alluding to political and social themes. *See p104.*

Terrace, Fundació Tàpies

Conjunt Monumental de la Plaça del Rei

Explore the medieval Palau Reial and wander among the splendid remains of Barcelona's Roman walls and waterways at the city's history museum. The museum is partly housed in the 15th-century Casa Padellàs on the impressive medieval Plaça del Rei. *See p71.*

Badge, FC Barcelona

Museu del FC Barcelona

This shrine to the city's football club draws a mind-boggling number of fans paying homage to their team. Trophies, posters and other memorabilia celebrate the club's 100-year history. Also visit the adjacent Camp Nou Stadium. *See p111.*

Museu Marítim

Barcelona's formidable sea-faring history is showcased in the cavernous, 13th-century Drassanes Reials (Royal Shipyards). The collection, which spans from the Middle Ages to the 19th century, includes a full-scale replica of the *Real*, the flagship galley of Don Juan of Austria, who led the Christians to victory against the Turks during the Battle of Lepanto in 1571. Also on display are model ships, maps and navigational instruments. *See p81.*

Museu Frederic Marès

Catalan sculptor Frederic Marès (1893–1991) was a passionate and eclectic collector. Housed here, under one roof,

are many remarkable finds amassed during his travels. Among the vast array of historical objects on display are Romanesque and Gothic religious art and sculptures, plus everything from dolls and fans to pipes and walking sticks.

Virgin, Museu Frederic Marès *See p72.*

CosmoCaixa Museu de la Ciencia

Exhibits covering the whole history of science, from the Big Bang to the computer age, are housed in this modern museum. Highlights include an interactive tour of the geological history of our planet, an area of real Amazonian rain forest, and a planetarium. ◈ *Teodor Roviralta 47–51* • Map B1 • Open 10am–8pm Tue–Sun • Adm (free first and last Sun of month) • DA • www.cosmocaixa.com

Top 10 Quirky Museums/Monuments

1 Museu de Carrosses Fúnebres
Late 19th-century hearses reveal how *Barcelonins* of the past met their maker. ◈ *C/Sancho d'Àvila 2* • Map G3

2 Museu de l'Eròtica
A historical overview of sex from Kama Sutra drawings to salacious posters. ◈ *La Rambla 96* • Map L3

3 Museu de la Màgia
A museum devoted to magic, with a collection dating from the 18th century. ◈ *Carrer Oli 6* • Map N4

4 Museu dels Autòmates
A colourful museum of human and animal automatons. ◈ *Parc d'Atraccions del Tibidabo* • Map B1

5 Museu de la Xocolata
A celebration of chocolate, with interactive exhibits, edible city models and tastings. ◈ *Pl Pons i Clerch* • Map P4

6 Museu de Cera
Over 350 wax figures, from Marilyn Monroe to Franco and Gaudí. ◈ *Ptge de la Banca 7* • Map L5

7 Museu del Calçat
Footwear from all ages, including shoes worn by famous folks. ◈ *Pl de Sant Felip Neri 5* • M3

8 Museu del Perfum
Hundreds of perfume bottles from Roman times to the present. ◈ *Pg de Gràcia 39* • E2

9 Cap de Barcelona
Pop artist, Roy Lichtenstein's "Barcelona Head" (1992). ◈ *Pg de Colom* • Map N5

10 Peix
Frank Gehry's huge shimmering fish sculpture (1992). ◈ *Port Olímpic* • Map G5

Many museums are free one day a month **See p140**

Left **Cafè de l'Òpera, La Rambla** Right **Waterside dining, Port Vell**

🔟 Cafés & Light Bites

Cafè Zurich
This sprawling *Modernista* café can be summed up in three words: location, location, location. Dominating a corner of the city's hub, Plaça de Catalunya, this buzzing meeting point is packed at all hours with locals and visitors sipping coffees and cocktails. ◈ *Pl de Catalunya 1 • Map M1*

Cafè de l'Òpera
Kick back at this elegant, late 19th-century café while rubbing shoulders with a mixed crowd, tended to by vested *cambrers* (waiters). This former *xocolateria* (confectionary café) – named after the Liceu opera house opposite – still serves fine gooey delights such as *xurros amb xocolata* (strips of fried dough with thick chocolate). It is near to perfect for people-watching on La Rambla. ◈ *La Rambla 74 • Map L4*

Cafè Zurich, Plaça de Catalunya

Tèxtil Cafè
Nestled in a sun-splashed medieval courtyard, this soothing café offers cheery respite from the outside world. Tuck into the *amanida tèxtil*, with goat's cheese, artichokes and leafy greens, or international fusion favourites, from *baba ganoush* to couscous. ◈ *C/Montcada 12 • Map P4 • Closed Mon, Tue eve, Wed eve & Thu eve in winter*

Bar-Restaurant Hivernacle
Pause in the glass-topped, 19th-century Hivernacle after a saunter through Parc de la Ciutadella *(see pp16–17)* to sip iced coffee or chilled *cava* amid the moist, fragrant warmth of tropical plants. Fresh nibbles include grilled squid, anchovies and sandwiches, including one with pungent Manchego cheese. ◈ *Pg Picasso • Map Q4 • Closed Sun eve and for occasional events*

Cafè-Bar del Pi
Round off your Barri Gòtic ramble with *una copa* (alcoholic drink) and *una xerrada* (chat) on this café's enticing terrace. The café's small interior also packs in the lively crowd. *See p78.*

Bar Kasparo
This laid-back, outdoor café serves a sprightly menu of fresh, international fare with an Asiatic twist, including chicken curry and Greek salad. After the sun dips beneath the horizon, a bar-like vibe takes over, fuelled by beer and cider. ◈ *Pl Vicenç Martorell 4 • Map L2*

 All food and drink names are given in Catalan, but in many cases the Castilian variant is used just as commonly.

Café Salambó

Stylish evidence of Gràcia's intellectual and literary character, this airy, lofty café draws arty locals. While away the afternoon over a steaming *cafè amb llet* or munching on fresh salads and *entrepans* (sandwiches). *See p115.*

Café Salambó

Laie Llibreria Cafè

Tuck into a generous buffet of rice, pasta, greens, chicken and more at this charming, long-running Eixample café-bookshop. Or opt for the well-priced vegetarian menu, including soup, salad and a main dish. An elegant, but informal, any time of the day option. *See p108.*

Granja Dulcinea

The *xocolateries* and *granjes* along Carrer Petritxol *(see p74)* have been satiating sugar cravings for decades. Among them is this old-fashioned café with to-die-for delights, from *xurros amb xocolata* to strawberries and whipped cream. In the summer, *orxates* and *granissats* are on the menu. ❧ *C/Petritxol 2 • Map L3 • Closes at 9pm*

El Bosc de les Fades

Enter this dark, surreal, fairy-tale-like café, replete with faux gnarled trees, intimate cosy nooks and a gurgling brook, to enjoy delicious coffee concoctions, cocktails, wine and beer. ❧ *Ptge de la Banca • Map L5*

Top 10 Café Drinks

Cafè amb llet
Traditionally enjoyed in the morning, *cafè amb llet* is an ample cup of milky coffee.

Tallat & Cafè Sol
Need a fortifying caffeine fix? Try a *tallat*, a small cup of coffee with a dash of milk. A *cafè sol* is just plain coffee. In the summer, opt for either one *amb gel* (with ice).

Cigaló
For coffee with a bite, try a *cigaló (carajillo)*, which has a shot of alcohol, usually *conyac* (cognac), *whisky* or *rom* (rum).

Orxata
This sweet, milky-white drink made from a tuber (tiger nut) is a summertime favourite.

Granissat
Slake your thirst with a cool *granissat*, a crushed-ice drink, usually lemon flavoured.

Aigua
Stay hydrated with *aigua mineral* (mineral water) – *amb gas* is sparkling, *sense gas*, still.

Cacaolat
Chocolate lovers swoon over this chocolate-milk concoction, one of Spain's most popular sweet drink exports.

Una Canya & Una Clara
Una canya is roughly a quarter of a litre of *cervesa de barril* (draft beer). *Una clara* is the same, but with fizzy lemonade mixed in.

Cava
Catalonia's answer to champagne is its home-grown *cava*, of which Freixenet and Codorníu are the most famous brands.

Sangría
This ever-popular concoction of red wine, fruit juices, and liquors is ordered at cafés throughout the city.

Left **Flash Flash** Right **Tragaluz**

Best Restaurants & Tapas Bars

Cal Pep
The line-up at this traditional, boisterous tapas bar includes top-notch cured hams and sausages, *truita de patates* (potato omelette), fresh *mariscs* (shellfish) and an array of daily tapas specials, depending on what's at the market. *See p79.*

Tragaluz
By day, the eye-catching *tragaluz* (skylight) showers light over the playful interior (designed by Barcelona's favourite designer, Javier Mariscal); by night, you can dine under the stars. The menu tempts with Mediterranean cuisine, such as pasta with asparagus and fresh lobster. *See p109.*

El Asador d'Aranda
This palatial restaurant, perched high above the city on Tibidabo, dishes up the best in Castilian cuisine. Sizeable starters include *pica pica*, a tasty array of sausages, peppers and hams. The signature main dish is *lechazo* (young lamb) roasted in a wood-fired oven. *See p117.*

Wall tile advertising Barcelona restaurant

Agua
A classy, waterfront gem with an inviting outdoor terrace, Agua serves prime Mediterranean cuisine and fresh seafood, including a particularly excellent *carpaccio de rapè* (monkfish). *See p101.*

Can Culleretes
This cosy spot, with its wood-beamed ceilings, is the second oldest restaurant in Spain (dating from 1796). Photos of famous folks who have had their fill of the hearty Catalan cuisine line the walls. Try the goose with apples or the duck with prunes. ⓢ *C/Quintana 5 • Map L4 • 93 317 30 22 • Closed Sun eve, Mon & Jul • €€*

Bar Ra
A funky, flower-filled oasis in El Raval, this juice-bar-café-restaurant is the place for organic, multi-cultural cuisine. Start your day with muesli or muffins and a fresh papaya or pear juice. The lunch and dinner menu might include Japanese tofu, Peruvian *ceviche* (raw seafood marinated in lemon) or a Cuban chicken and mango chutney dish. *See p87.*

Els Quatre Gats
The legendary haunt of Picasso and his cronies, this late 19th-century bar-restaurant once hosted many a pastis-fuelled night among the city's bohemian crowd. Hearty Catalan and

Paella

All food and drink names are given in Catalan, but in many cases the Castilian variant is used just as commonly.

Mediterranean fare is enjoyed amid replicas of works by the artists who found inspiration here. ۞ C/Montsió 3 • Map 2 • 93 302 41 40 • €€€

Casa Leopoldo

This comfortable, family-run restaurant serves some of the finest Catalan cuisine in the city. Fresh seafood is the highlight, with innovative platters of *bacallà* (salt cod), *llenguado* (sole) and *gambes* (prawns). *See p87.*

Bar-Restaurante Can Tomàs

A cheap, no-nonsense tapas bar in the uptown area of Sarrià. Every tapas-lover knows that the city's best *patates braves* and *patates amb alioli* are found here. Ask for the *doble mixta* to sample both. *See p117.*

Outdoor terrace, Bar Ra

Flash Flash

Settle in to a leatherette seat at this groovy 1960s retro diner and gorge on hefty *truites* (omelettes) with all manner of fillings, from chicken and bechamel to fried bread, cheese and tomato. For dessert, the adventurous dig into an array of sweet *truites*, including a fluffy omelette stuffed with chunks of fried, sweetened apples and drizzled in sweet syrup. *See p117.*

Top 10 Tapas

1 Patates Braves
This traditional tapas favourite consists of fried potatoes topped with a spicy sauce. Equally tasty are *patates* heaped with *alioli* (garlic mayonnaise).

2 Calamars
A savoury seafood option is *calamars* (squid) *a la romana* (deep-fried in batter) or *a la planxa* (grilled).

3 Pa amb Tomàquet
A key part of any tapas spread is this bread topped with tomato and olive oil.

4 Croquetes
A perennial favourite are croquettes; tasty fried morsels of bechamel, usually with ham, chicken or tuna.

5 Musclos o Escopinyes
Sample Barcelona's fruits of the sea with tapas of tasty mussels or cockles.

6 Truita de Patates
The most common tapas dish is this thick potato omelette, often topped with *alioli*.

7 Ensaladilla Russa
This "Russian salad" includes potatoes, onions, tuna (and often peas, carrots and other vegetables), all generously enveloped in mayonnaise.

8 Gambes al'allet
An appetizing dish of fried prawns (shrimp) coated in garlic and olive oil.

9 Pernil Serrà
Cured ham is a Spanish obsession. The best, and most expensive, is Extremadura's speciality, Jabugo.

10 Fuet
Embotits (Catalan sausages) include the ever-popular *fuet*, a dry, flavourful variety, most famously produced in the Catalonian town of Vic.

Bar interior, Zona Alta

Night-time Hot Spots

Mirablau

Look down on the glittering Barcelona cityscape from this stylish bar perched atop Tibidabo. Once you've drunk in the view (and a cocktail or two), head downstairs to the dance club and groove to tunes from the 1970s and '80s, with some current Spanish pop favourites thrown into the mix. *See p116.*

Marsella

Founded in 1820, this atmospheric throwback, run by the fifth generation of the Lamiel family, sits in the heart of the Barri Xinès *(see p82)*. Marsella is one of the few places in town where you can enjoy the potent drink absinthe *(absenta)*. Settle in at one of the wrought-iron *Modernista* tables, surrounded by ancient mirrors and old religious statues, and test your mettle with the potent yellow liquor that is specially bottled for the bar. *See p86.*

Decoration, Barcelona bar

Otto Zutz

A swanky Barcelona night-life institution, this three-storey disco is on the itinerary for well-heeled media types. The music verges on the main-stream, with big-name DJs spinning everything from techno to contemporary favourites. *See p116.*

Mond Bar

This tiny, trendy bar in the heart of Gràcia is a magnet for mellow bar-flies who come to mingle, smoke and listen to DJ-spun tunes, including techno, pop, soul and 1970s classics. *See p116.*

Salvation

Pulsating near the "Gay-xample" – a section of the lower Eixample that is dotted with gay bars and clubs – is this see-and-be-seen nightspot. It's always jam-packed with a dance-driven crowd of scantily clad, beautiful men cruising for a connection. The two large dance rooms vibrate to the beat of techno, and music from the 1970s, '80s and '90s, played by local and international DJs. Ⓢ *C/Ronda Sant Pere 19–21 • Map N1 • Open Fri–Sat • Adm • DA*

La Terrrazza

Located inside the Poble Espanyol *(see p91)*, La Terrrazza is one of the most popular summer nightclubs in Barcelona. The patio becomes the dance-floor, the porches are bars and

Gin Martinis, Mirablau

For tips on drinking and standard opening hours See p138 & p140

the garden provides a refreshing chill-out area. ◈ Poble Espanyol, Av Marquès de Comillas • Map A3 • Open Thu–Sun (May–Sep) • Adm

El Cafè que pone Muebles Navarro

One of the pioneers in the revival of the El Raval *barrio*, this spacious lounge bar serves up cocktails and light bites to a hip, eclectic crowd. With a nod to its former life as an old furniture shop, the minimalist space is scattered with comfortable, mismatched second-hand sofas and chairs. *See p86.*

Inside Razzmatazz, Port Olímpic Party Strip

La Pedrera de Nit

If Gaudí's undulating Pedrera rooftop *(see pp20–21)* looks surreal by day, experience it at night for full effect. On Friday and Saturday evenings between mid-June and late July, La Pedrera opens up its magical rooftop for a night of live music and *cava* drinking. Wander among Gaudí's mosaic chimneys, illuminated against the night sky, while enjoying jazz, flamenco fusion or tango. ◈ C/Provença 261–265 • Map E2 • Reservations essential: call 902 10 12 12 • Adm • DA

Jamboree

Venture underground – quite literally – to this popular, hopping jazz club-cum-nightclub in a vaulted space beneath Plaça Reial. Nightly live jazz sessions kick off around 11pm. DJs take over later with dance-inducing sounds. *See p77.*

Jamboree

Port Olímpic Party Strip

Come nightfall – and well into the early hours of the morning – the Port Olímpic turns into a massive dance party, its long string of clubs and bars *(see p100)* booming everything from techno to salsa, Spanish pop to more techno. Club-hop your way down the strip and sip overpriced cocktails on the outdoor terraces before joining the sweaty, gyrating dance crowds inside. Entry into the bars and clubs along the strip is free, and most start getting lively after 10pm, staying open until 3am, 5am or later. ◈ Moll de Mèstral • Map G5

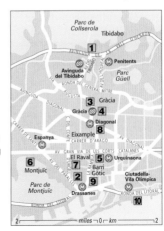

For more bars & clubs in the old town See pp76–7 & p86

Left **Club scene, Sitges** Right **Restaurante Castro**

Gay & Lesbian Hang-outs

1 Antinous Llibreria-Cafè
Antinous is a popular, gay meeting point just off the southern end of La Rambla. The café incorporates a spacious shop, stocking gifts, books and videos, and has a small bar area with exhibitions. Pick up a copy of *Nois*, a free magazine available in most gay venues, which gives the lowdown on the gay scene. ◈ *C/Josep Anselm Clavé 6 • Map L6 • Closed Sun • DA*

Party-goers, Free Girls

2 Dietrich Gay Teatro Café
A gay venue with a mixed door policy, Dietrich is a trendy club with attractive golden walls and an internal garden. As well as playing house and garage music, it features performances by drag artists, dancers and acrobats. ◈ *Consell de Cent 255 • Map D3*

3 Restaurante Castro
This ultra-chic restaurant offers hefty portions of Mediterranean cuisine with an exotic twist. The heavy duty decor of industrial-style black chains and metal is toned down by soft lighting and relaxing music. Make a reservation, as this is

one of the most popular gay restaurants in town. ◈ *C/Casanova 85 • Map D2 • 93 323 67 84 • Closed Sat lunch & Sun • €€€€ • DA*

4 Sauna Galilea
Barcelona's newest gay sauna (for men only) is ultra-clean, with four floors offering Turkish baths, Jacuzzis and saunas, as well as a bar and internet service. There are also private cabins, some with video players.
◈ *C/Calábria 59 • Map C3 • Adm*

5 Zeltas
One of the hottest club-bars in town, Zeltas has trendy decor, in the style of a loft apartment, and really pulls in the crowds. A heady mix of testosterone, potent drinks and pumping house makes this a prime spot to mingle with some Barcelona beauties. ◈ *C/Casanova 75 • Map D3 • Occasional adm*

Books, Antinous Llibería-Cafè

 b-guided **(see p134)** *is available from selected stores and venues; it gives more information on gay-friendly restaurants, bars and shops.*

Eagle
Anything goes at the city's most hardcore gay club, even nudity is permitted, welcomed, in fact, if it comes adorned with S&M gear. Be warned: this place is described by the locals as *morboso* (morbid). Things get going around midnight, and you're unlikely to go home alone. ◊ Pg St Joan 152 • Map F2 • Adm after 11pm

Metro
Metro has two dance floors, one playing house, while the other has a free-and-easy music policy and a pool table. The club only livens up around 2am. You can pick up free tickets at nearby Dietrich restaurant, another gay haunt. ◊ C/Sepúlveda 185 • Map J1 • Adm • DA

Free Girls
This classic, lesbian hangout is a booming club with beautiful bodies and fantastic dance music. Ultra-chilled surroundings mean it's easy to make acquaintances. The door policy is strictly female only. ◊ C/Marià Cubí 4 • Map E1 • Occasional adm • Closed Mon–Wed

Punto BCN
For over 10 years, this relaxed, friendly bar has stayed in vogue on a fickle gay scene. It gets impossibly busy around midnight at weekends and the music is loud, but it's a good place to get fired up for a night out and get the latest on what else is happening in town. ◊ C/Muntaner 63 • Map D3 • DA

Beaches
In summer, gay men gather for some sun, fun and plenty of posing in front of the Club de Natació Barcelona on Barceloneta beach near Plaça del Mar. ◊ Map E6

Top 10 Gay Hot Spots in Sitges

XXL
Popular with the in-crowd, with nice decor, a good drinks selection and techno music. ◊ C/Joan Tarrida 7

El Candil
This classic disco bar is always busy, busy, busy. ◊ Carreta 9

El Mediterráneo
A visit to this multi-space bar is a must for its original design. ◊ C/St Bonaventura 6

Trailer
Sitges' oldest gay disco is always packed with friendly faces. ◊ C/Àngel Vidal 36 • Adm

Organic
Organic is a new disco on the gay scene, frequented by a fashion-industry crowd. ◊ C/Bonaire 15 • Adm

Beaches
The beach in front of the Hotel Calípolis in Sitges' centre is a gay magnet, as is the nudist one on the way to the town of Vilanova.

Night-time Cruising
The pier just past Hotel Calípolis is one of the busiest cruising spots. Prime time is between 3am and dawn.

Miami
Keen prices and a friendly atmosphere make this restaurant a Sitges favourite. ◊ C/St Pau 11 • 93 894 02 06

Dive
This shop has a fabulous, if rather expensive, selection of gay clothing and accessories. ◊ C/St Francesc 33

El Hotel Romàntic
A simple, unpretentious gay-friendly hotel, with a pretty garden. ◊ C/St Isidre 33 • 93 894 83 75 • www.hotel romantic.com

The "Gayxample" around the intersection of C/Casanova and C/Diputació, is the heart of Barcelona's gay scene.

Left **Handbags, Avinguda Diagonal** Right **Shop front, Passeig de Gràcia**

Best Shopping Areas

Passeig de Gràcia
Barcelona's grand avenue of lavish *Modernista* buildings is fittingly home to the city's premier fashion and design stores. From the international big league (Chanel, Hermès, Swatch) to Spain's heavy hitters (Loewe, Zara, Mango; *see p139*), it's all here. And topping the interior design list is the perennially popular Vinçon *(see p106)*. Side streets reveal more sublime shopping, notably Carrer Consell de Cent, which is dotted with art galleries, and carrers Mallorca, València and Roselló. ✆ *Map E3*

Bulevard Rosa & Bulevard dels Antiquaris
Opened in 1978, Barcelona's first fashion mall, Bulevard Rosa, is still one of its classiest, with over 100 shops showcasing clothes, shoes and accessories by Spanish and international designers. The adjoining Bulevard dels Antiquaris is a spacious mall, with over 60 antiques and arts shops. ✆ *Bulevard Rosa: Pg de Gràcia 53 • Map E2 • Open 10:30am–9pm Mon–Sat* ✆ *Bulevard dels Antiquaris: Pg de Gràcia 55–57 • Map E2 • Open 10:30am–8:30pm Mon–Sat*

Plaça de Catalunya & Carrer Pelai
The city's booming centrepiece is also its commercial crossroads, flanked by the department store El Corte Inglés and the shopping mall El Triangle, which includes FNAC (books, CDs, videos) and Séphora (perfumes and cosmetics). Lined with shoe and clothing shops, the nearby Carrer Pelai is said to have more pedestrian traffic than any other shopping street in Spain. ✆ *El Corte Inglés: Pl de Catalunya 14 • Map M1 • Open 10am–10pm Mon–Sat* ✆ *El Triangle: C/Pelai 39 • Map L1 • Open 10am–10pm Mon–Sat*

Portal de l'Àngel
Once a Roman thoroughfare leading into the walled city of Barcino, today the pedestrian street of Portal de l'Àngel is traversed by hordes of shoppers toting bulging bags. The street is chock-full of shoe, clothing, jewellery and accessory shops. ✆ *Map M2*

Rambla de Catalunya
The genteel, classier extension of La Rambla, this well-maintained

Shopping crowds, Portal de l'Àngel

street offers a refreshing change from its cousin's more down-at-heel carnival atmosphere. Chic shops and cafés, as well as their moneyed customers, pepper the street's length, from Plaça de Catalunya to Diagonal. You'll find everything from fine footwear and leather bags to linens and lamps. 🅢 *Map E2*

Storefront, Carrer Portaferrisa

Avinguda Diagonal
Big and brash, traffic-choked Diagonal is hard to miss, a cacophonous avenue that cuts, yes, diagonally across the entire city. It is a premier shopping street, particularly west of Passeig de Gràcia to its culmination in L'Illa mall and the large El Corte Inglés department store near Plaça Maria Cristina. Lining this long stretch is a host of high-end clothing and shoe stores (Armani, Gucci and Versace among them), interior design shops, jewellery and watch purveyors, and more. 🅢 *Map D1*

Carrer Portaferrissa
From zebra platform shoes to bellybutton rings and pastel baby T-shirts, this street's other name could well be Carrer "Trendy". Along this strip you'll find El Mercadillo *(see p75)* mini-mall, crammed with hip little shops selling spiked belts, frameless sunglasses, surf wear and the like. Just off this street is Galeries Maldà, Barcelona's first shopping gallery, with a range of shops and a cinema showing original-version independent and Bollywood films *(see p67)*. 🅢 *Galeries Maldà: Pl del Pi 1 • Map M3 • Open 10am–1:30pm & 4–8pm Mon–Sat*

Gràcia
Old bookstores, family-run *botigues de comestibles* (grocery stores) and bohemian shops selling Indian clothing and accessories cluster along Carrer Astúries (and its side streets) and along Travessera de Gràcia. A string of contemporary clothing and shoe shops also lines Gran de Gràcia. 🅢 *Map F1*

El Born
Amid El Born's web of streets are all sorts of art and design shops. Passeig del Born and Carrer Rec are dotted with innovative little galleries (from sculpture to interior design), plus clothing and shoe boutiques. 🅢 *Map P4*

La Maquinista
Housed in a converted locomotive factory in the Barri de Sant Andreu is Barcelona's gleaming new shopping complex. The mall offers everything under one roof, with over 200 shops, a multiplex cinema, a bowling alley and fast-food eateries galore. 🅢 *Pg de Potosí 2, 4 km E city centre • Off map • Open 10am–10pm Mon–Sat*

Produce, Mercat de Santa Caterina

Most Fascinating Markets

Mercat de La Boqueria
Barcelona's most famous food market is conveniently located on La Rambla *(see pp12–13)*. Freshness reigns supreme and shoppers are spoiled for choice, with hundreds of stalls selling everything from vine-ripened tomatoes to haunches of beef and moist wedges of Manchego cheese. The city's seaside status is in full evidence at the fish stalls. ◈ *La Rambla 91 • Map L3 • 7am–8pm Mon–Sat*

Els Encants
Barcelona's best flea market, Els Encants (east of the city) is where you'll find everything you want, from second-hand clothes, electrical appliances and toys to home-made pottery and used books. Discerning browsers can fit out an entire kitchen from an array of pots and pans. Bargain-hunters should come early. The market may move to the Plaça Monumental (bullring) in 2008. ◈ *Pl de les Glòries Catalanes • Map H3 • 8am–5:30pm Mon, Wed, Fri & Sat*

Fira de Santa Llúcia
The Christmas season is officially under way when local artisans set up shop outside the Cathedral for the annual Christmas fair. Well worth a visit if only to peruse the row upon row of *caganers*, miniature figures squatting to *fer caca* (take a poop). Uniquely Catalan, the *caganers* are usually hidden in the back of nativity scenes. This unusual celebration of the scatological also appears in other Christmas traditions. ◈ *Pl de la Seu • Map N3 • 1–23 Dec: 10am–8pm (times may vary) daily*

Book & Coin Market at Mercat de Sant Antoni
For book lovers, there's no better way to spend Sunday morning than browsing at this market (west of the city). You'll find a mind-boggling assortment of weathered paperbacks, ancient tomes, stacks of old magazines, comics, postcards and lots more, from coins to videos. ◈ *C/Comte d'Urgell • Map D2 • 8am–3pm Sun*

Fira de Santa Llúcia, Plaça de la Seu

Fira Artesana, Plaça del Pi

The Plaça del Pi *(see p37)* brims with natural and organic foods during the Fira Artesana, when producers bring their goods to this corner of the Barri Gòtic. The market specializes in home-made cheeses and honey – from clear clover honey from the Pyrenees to nutty concoctions from Morella. ⊗ *Pl del Pi • Map M3 • 10am–2pm & 5–9pm 1st & 3rd Fri, Sat & Sun of month*

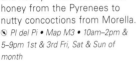

Cheeses, Fira Artesana, Plaça del Pi

Fira de Numismàtica

Spread out in the elegant Plaça Reial *(see p72)*, this popular stamp and coin market draws avid collectors from all over the city. The newest collectors' items are phone cards and old *xapes de cava* (cava bottle cork foils). When the market ends (and the local police go to lunch), a makeshift flea market takes over. Old folks from the barrio and immigrants haul out their belongings – old lamps, clothing, junk – and lay it all out on cloths on the ground. ⊗ *Pl Reial • Map L4 • 9:30am–2:30pm Sun*

Mercat de la Concepció

In the heart of the Eixample is this large market, renowned for its flowers. Blooming bouquets at the entrance offer a fragrant welcome to the bright flower stalls that lie within. ⊗ *C/València at C/Bruc • Map F2 • 8am–2:30pm Mon & Sat, 8am–8:30pm Tue–Fri*

Mercat de Santa Caterina

Each barrio has its own food market with tempting displays but this one boasts a spectacular setting. Opened in 2005, the new building was designed by Catalan architect Enric Miralles (1955–2000). ⊗ *Av Francesc Cambó 16 • Map N3 • 8am–2pm Mon, 8am–3:30pm Tue, Wed & Sat, 8am–8:30pm Thu & Fri*

Mercat del Art de la Plaça de Sant Josep Oriol

At weekends, local artists flock to this Barri Gòtic square to sell their art and set up their easels. You'll find everything from watercolours of Catalan landscapes to oil paintings of churches and castles. ⊗ *Pl de Sant Josep Oriol • Map M4 • 11am–8:30pm Sat, 10am–2pm Sun*

Mercat dels Antiquaris

Antiques aficionados and collectors contentedly rummage through jewellery, watches, candelabras, silver trays, embroidery and assorted bric-a-brac at this long-running antiques market in front of the Cathedral. ⊗ *Pl de la Seu • Map N3 • 10am–3pm Thu*

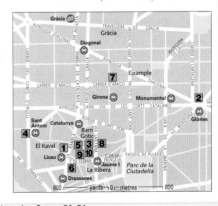

For more on shopping See pp50–51

Left **City vista, Mirador de Colom** Right **Gargoyles and view, Sagrada Família**

🔟 City Views

1 Tibidabo

The mountain of Tibidabo is the best vantage point for a bird's-eye view of Barcelona. Thrill-seekers opt for a spin on the Tibidabo fairground attraction *(see p111)* called La Atalaya, a rickety basket attached to an ancient crane-like contraption which gives a 360-degree view of Barcelona, the sea and the Pyrenees. A less giddy option is the Torre de Collserola *(see p111)* with its transparent lift rising up 288 m (945 ft). And for those who wish to keep their feet firmly on solid ground – cocktail in hand – settle in at the Mireblau bar *(see p 116)*.

2 Castell de Montjuïc

Montjuïc offers myriad viewpoints. The best is from the castle and gardens with their superb panoramas over the port and the city. Take the cable car up to the castle and walk down through ever-changing vistas to the Bar Miramar *(see p95)* for a refreshing drink. *See p89.*

Barcelona from Castell de Montjuïc

3 Les Golondrines & Orsom Catamaran

The sea offers a less vertiginous view of the cityscape. Glide out of the harbour on the pleasure boats known as *golondrines* or try the exhilarating trip under sail on an enormous catamaran. Both trips offer ample views of the city and of the new Port Olímpic area. See p133. ⊗ *Les Golondrines, Portal de la Pau • Map L6 • Call 93 442 31 06 for times • www.lasgolondrinas. com* ⊗ *Orsom Catamaran, Portal de la Pau • Map L6 • Call 93 441 05 37 for times • www.barcelona-orsom.com*

4 Cable Cars

The swaying cable cars that glide slowly between the Port and Montjuïc are something of a Barcelona landmark. To those not afraid of heights, they reveal hidden aspects of the city and provide a pleasurable way to get to the top of Montjuïc. *See p133.* ⊗ *Miramar, Montjuïc/Port de Barcelona • Map C5, D6 & E6 • Open 11am–9pm daily • Adm*

5 Mirador de Colom

At the end of La Rambla, the statue of Christopher Columbus offers a good vantage point for viewing the city. The column, rising 80 m (262 ft), was built in 1888. The elevator that whisks visitors to the top has, fortunately, been renovated since then! ⊗ *La Rambla/Drassanes • Map L6 • Open Jun–Sep: 9am–8:30pm daily; Oct–May: 10am–6:30pm daily • Adm €2.50*

Sagrada Família

When work first began, Gaudí's magical church lay on the outskirts of the city and Barcelona would have been just a shadow in the distance. A hundred years on, the church is located in the heart of the Eixample and the bell towers offer dizzying vistas of the entire city. An added bonus are the wonderful close-ups of the extraordinary Sagrada Família itself. See pp8–11.

View of the city and Casa-Museu Gaudí, Parc Güell

El Corte Inglés

The top floor of this department store has a glass-fronted cafeteria and restaurant with a terrace – an excellent place to lunch or just have a coffee. From here there are views of the nearby Plaça de Catalunya, the old town and the Eixample. The enormous store below stocks just about anything you might need to buy. ◎ Pl de Catalunya 14 • Map M1 • Free • DA

Parc Güell

In the north of the city, Gaudí's monumental Modernista park presents spectacular views across Barcelona and out to the Mediterranean from its various terraced levels. Trees and patches of woodland act as welcome shade from the fierce summer sun. See p112.

Barcelona Cathedral

From the heart of the Barri Gòtic, the Cathedral rooftop offers one of the least changed vistas in the city. Look out over the ramshackle rooftops – some dating to the 12th century – and the narrow alleys that spill out in all directions. There is a small charge for the elevator to the top. See pp14–15.

Helicopter Rides

For a bird's-eye view of Barcelona, consider a helicopter ride over the city. Helipistas SL will take a minimum of 2 people on a 30-minute ride over Montjuïc, the port and the southern part of the city. Transport to and from the out-of-town airport is included in the price. ◎ Pick up from any city centre location • call 93 730 49 11 or check www.helipistas.com for more information • Adm • DA

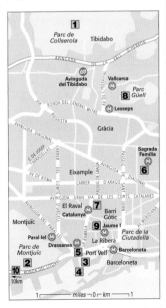

Barcelona's Top 10

Left **Barceloneta beach** Right **Parc de Joan Miró**

⑧⑩ Parks & Beaches

1 Parc de la Ciutadella

Barcelona's largest landscaped park offers a serene antidote to city life. Once the location of the 18th-century military citadel, this lovely 19th-century park is now home to the zoo, the Catalan parliament, two museums and a boating lake. There is an inviting café in the Hivernacle (winter greenhouse), which hosts occasional live music. *See pp16–17.*

2 Parc Güell

Originally conceived as a suburban estate to the north of the city, Parc Güell is like a surreal, Asian terraced farm. Twisting pathways and avenues of columned arches blend in with the hillside, playfully fusing nature and fantasy. The esplanade, with its stunning, curved, mosaic bench, is the park's centrepiece. From here

Cascade Fountain, Parc de la Ciutadella

there are spectacular views *(see p55)* of the entire city and of the fairy-tale gatehouses below. Gaudí's former home is now the Casa-Museu Gaudí. *See p112.*

3 Jardins del Laberint d'Horta

These enchanting Neo-Classical gardens date back to 1791, making this elegant park one of the oldest in the city. Situated up above the city, where the air is cooler and cleaner, the park includes themed gardens, waterfalls and a small canal. The highlight is the enormous maze, which has a statue of Eros at its centre. *See p113.*

4 Parc de Cervantes

Built in 1964 to celebrate 25 years of Franco rule, this beautiful park on the outskirts of town would have been more appropriately named Park of the Roses. There are over 11,000 rose bushes of 245 varieties; when in bloom, their aroma pervades the park. People pour in at weekends, but the park is blissfully deserted during the week. ⊗ *Av Diagonal • Off map*

5 Jardins de Pedralbes

These picturesque gardens lie just in front of the former Palau Reial (royal palace) of Pedralbes – now home to the Museu de Ceràmica and Museu de les Arts Decoratives *(see p112)*. Under the shade of an enormous eucalyptus tree and near a small bamboo forest is a fountain by Gaudí,

56

All the city parks are officially open from around 10am until dusk.

which was only discovered in 1983.
⊗ Av Diagonal 686
• Off map

6 Parc de Joan Miró

Also know as Parc de l'Escorxador, this park was built on the site of a 19th-century slaughter-house (*excorxador*). Dominating the paved upper level of the park is Miró's striking 22-m (72-ft)

Parc de l'Espanya Industrial

sculpture, *Dona i Ocell (Woman and Bird*; 1983). Elsewhere there are three children's play areas set around a café. ⊗ C/Tarragona
• Map B2

7 Parc de l'Espanya Industrial

Built on the site of a former textiles factory, this modern park, by Basque architect Luis Peña Ganchegui, has deteriorated somewhat since its inauguration in 1985. It still has a certain appeal, including ten strange lighthouse-style towers that line the boating lake and an enormous cast-iron dragon, which doubles as a slide. There's a good terrace bar with a playground for the kids. ⊗ Pl de Joan Peiró • Off map

8 City Beaches

The beaches of Barcelona were once insalubrious areas to be avoided. With the 1992 Olympics they underwent a radical face-lift and today the stretches of Barceloneta and the Port Olímpic are a major people magnet. Just a short hop on the metro from the city centre, they provide the perfect opportunity for a refreshing Mediterranean dip. The beaches are regularly

cleaned and the many facilities include showers, toilets, childrens' play areas, volleyball nets and an open-air gym. There are boats and surfboards for rent. Be warned: bag snatching is endemic. *See p97*.

9 Castelldefels

Just 20 km (12 miles) south of Barcelona are 5 km (3 miles) of wide, sandy beaches with shallow waters. Beach bars entice week-end sun worshippers out of the afternoon sun for long, lazy sea-food lunches and jugs of sangria aplenty. Windsurfers and pedalos are for hire. ⊗ Off map • Train to Platja de Castelldefels from Estació de Sants or Passeig de Gràcia

10 Premià/El Masnou

By far the best beaches within easy reach of Barcelona, just 20 km (12 miles) to the north, these two adjoining beaches lure locals with gorgeous golden sand and clear, blue waters. ⊗ Train to Premià or El Masnou from Plaça de Catalunya or Estació de Sants

Left **La Rambla** Right **Cyclist, Passeig Marítim**

Top10 Walks & Bike Rides

La Rambla & The Port
From Plaça de Catalunya, stroll the length of Barcelona's most famous street, La Rambla *(see pp12–13)*, stopping en route to enjoy the street performances. Turn left at the port and admire the luxury yachts as you follow the water round to Barceloneta. Continue along Pg Joan de Borbó and turn left down any of the side streets that lead to the sand and sea. ◈ *Map M1*

Barri Gòtic
Wandering this network of atmospheric, ancient streets is the best way to experience the old town. Take a short stretch of the busy C/Portaferrisa *(see p51)* from La Rambla and turn right down tiny C/Petritxol *(see p74)*, with its confectionery shops and jewellers, to the Església de Santa Maria del Pi. Continue down C/Rauric, left onto C/Ferran and up to Plaça de Sant Jaume *(see p71)*. Turn left onto C/Bisbe leading to Plaça de la Seu and the Cathedral *(see pp14–15)*. ◈ *Map L3*

Eixample
For some of the city's most breathtaking *Modernista* gems, walk the length of Pg de Gràcia south to north, past the Mansana de la Discòrdia *(see p103)* and La Pedrera *(see pp20–21)*. Turn right onto C/Mallorca, which leads to Gaudí's Sagrada Família *(see pp 8–11)*. Take a left along C/Marina, past the church's awe-inspiring Nativity Façade, and head up Av Gaudí to Hospital de la Santa Creu i de Sant Pau *(see p103)*. ◈ *Map E3*

Tibidabo
Get high above the city by following the gently climbing Av del Tibidabo from the FGC station. Then follow signposts to the right through the steep wooded park, Font del Racó, and continue until you arrive at Plaça Doctor Andreu with its terrace bars and panoramic city views. ◈ *Map B1*

Montjuïc
Take in the city's green scene with an amble around Montjuïc's verdant slopes. The initial climb

Parc de Collserola

The CCCB (see pp28–9) offers guided walks in English during the summer. For more on walking tours **See p133.**

to the grandiose Palau Nacional *(see pp18–19)* from Plaça d'Espanya is eased by a series of escalators. From the palace, veer left and continue along the main road, stopping off at Jardí Mossèn Jacint Verdaguer *(see p94)* before continuing round to Miramar for a spectacular view. ◈ *Map B3*

Backstreet, Barri Gòtic

Parc de Collserola
It's difficult to believe that this serene nature reserve lies just 10 minutes drive from the metropolis. Explore its delightful hiking, biking and nature trails on foot or by mountain bike. Take the funicular train to the top of Tibidabo and head towards the Torre de Collserola *(see p111)*, turning off on any one of the colour-coded woodland paths. A tourist information point provides maps and further information. ◈ *Tourist Info: Carretera de l'Església 92 • Map E3 • Open 9:30am–3pm daily*

Coastal Bike Ride
Breeze along the city's coastal cycle path and take in seaside Barcelona. Pick up the path from the bottom of La Rambla and follow it north to Barceloneta, where it runs along the beachfront, past the shiny new Port Olímpic as far as Platja de la Mar Bella. ◈ *Map B3*

Diagonal Bike Ride
From Pedralbes to the sea, this route along the city's most elegant boulevard gives you a clear idea of Barcelona's size. The tree-lined cycle path follows Diagonal; start at the top (Zona Universitària) and continuing through the new city of Diagonal Mar until you arrive on the other

side of the city just a stone's throw from the Besòs River. ◈ *Map A1*

Les Planes
Just a 15-minute *ferrocarril* ride from Plaça de Catalunya (in the direction of Sant Cugat) is the picturesque spot of Baixador de Valvidrera. Perfect for an out-of-town stroll, there is a steep path through the woods, which opens up into a beautiful, green valley. In summer, there are barbecue facilities where you can throw on your own steaks. ◈ *4 km N of Barcelona*

Costa Brava Coastal Path
At the end of the Platja de Sant Pol in Sant Feliu de Guíxols is the start of a beautiful, coastal path that winds north through shady tamarind trees with views of rocky coves and the Mediterranean. Around the headland and down a stairway, you will find the fabulous beach of Sa Conca, voted the sixth best in Spain. ◈ *75 km NE of Barcelona*

Left **Bernat Picornell outdoor pool** Right **Sunbathers, Platja de la Barceloneta**

🔟 Activities in Barcelona

1 Sunbathing & Swimming
Head to the city beaches
(see p57) to cool down and escape
the stifling heat. Barcelona boasts
a wide range of fabulous beaches,
from Barceloneta, lined with bars
and restaurants, to the reclaimed
beaches of Vila
Olímpica, Bogatell and
Mar Bella. 🔹 *Map F6–H6*

2 Watersports
A wide variety of
activities is on offer in
the jet-set surround-
ings of Port Olímpic
and neighbouring
beaches, including
dinghy sailing and
windsurfing. For the
experienced, boats are
available for hire from
the Escola Municipal de Vela; for
the beginner, there are classes.
Night-time kayaking tours of the
city's beaches are available from
Desconnecta. 🔹 *Escola Municipal
de vela • Moll de Gregal • Map G6 • 93
225 79 40 • Open 9:30am–8pm daily
🔹 Desconnecta • C/Ticia 42 • 93 417 93
62 • www.desconnecta.com*

Volleyball, Platja de Nova Icària

3 Swimming
Set in the green environs of
Montjuïc, the outstanding outdoor pool of Bernat Picornell is
surprisingly uncrowded, especially
in summer. Renovated for the
Olympics, it has sun loungers, an
ice-cream stall and a huge electronic timer for swimmers to time
their sprints. During the summer,
there's a film programme known

as "watch and swim". 🔹 *Av del
Estadi • Map A4 • Open 7am–midnight
Mon–Fri, 7am–9pm Sat, 7am–8:30pm
(4pm winter) Sun • Adm • DA*

4 Pitch-&-Putt Golf
The Costa Brava is emerging
as one of Spain's top
golf destinations, but
if you're looking to tee
off in town, your best
bets are the nearby
pitch-and-putt courses
in Badalona and Cas-
telldefels. 🔹 *Castell de
Godmar, Badalona, 5km NE
Barcelona • 93 395 27 79
• Open 8:30am–dusk daily
🔹 Canal Olímpic • Castelldefels, 20 km S Barcelona
• 93 636 28 96 • Open
9am–9pm Tue–Sun*

5 Beach Volleyball
On weekend mornings year-
round you can pick up a volleyball game at Platja de la Nova
Icària. It is best to go with enough
people to form a team, but you
are usually welcome to join in
an ongoing game. 🔹 *Map H5*

6 Weight Lifting
The sports centre in the
Parc de l'Espanya Industrial
(see p57) has excellent weight-
lifting facilities, a sauna, Turkish
bath, Jacuzzi, badminton courts
and a swimming pool. One-day
membership is available. 🔹*C/
Muntadas • Off map • 93 426 10 70
• Open 6am–11pm Mon–Fri, 8am–9pm
Sat, 8am–2:30pm Sun*

 *For more on Barcelona's parks & beaches **See pp56–7***

7 Rollerskating

Hire a pair of in-line skates from Desconnecta and breeze around Barcelona. Bikes and scooters are also available for rent from here. ◉ *Desconnecta • C/Ticia 42 • 93 417 93 62*

8 Pool & Billiards

Shoot some pool at Gràcia's lovely Cafè Salambó, where there are pool and billard tables for rent upstairs, not to mention good drinks, tasty food, a friendly ambience and a lively, arty crowd *(see p115)*.

9 Sardanes

These traditional Catalan dances *(see p65)* take place regularly all over the city and at most local festas. Far from being exclusive, they often involve up to 200 people and there's no reason why you can't be one of them. The tourist office *(see p134)* can provide information on these events.

10 Frontó

Egalitarian tennis or poor man's squash, all you need is a tennis racket and ball to beat against the wall to enjoy this popular pastime. The city's parks are full of free *frontó* courts; one of the best is next to the Casa del Mig in the Parc de l'Espanya Industrial *(see p57)*.

Rollerblader, Moll de la Barceloneta

Top 10 Spectator Sports & Events

1 FC Barcelona Football

Tickets to see this first-division side are rare; 4,000 are sold a week before matches – call to find out when to queue. ◉ *Sep–Jun • 93 496 36 00*

2 RCD Espanyol

It's easier to get tickets for this first-division football side; they play at Estadi Olímpic *(see p90)*. ◉ *Sep–Jun • 90 219 62 59*

3 FC Barcelona Basketball

The team of the city's second favourite sport play at the Palau Blaugrana. ◉ *Sep–May • 90 218 99 00*

4 FC Barcelona Hockey

Roller hockey (played on skates) is popular in Barcelona. ◉ *Oct–Apr • 90 218 99 00*

5 Torneo Conde de Godo

A tennis tournament that attracts some big names. ◉ *mid–late Apr • 93 203 78 52*

6 Cursa El Corte Inglés

A 11-km (7-mile) run with thousands of participants. ◉ *May or Jun • 93 306 38 00*

7 La Volta Ciclista de Catalunya

Cyclists warm up for the more serious European events with this testing route. ◉ *late May– Jun • 93 431 82 98*

8 Montmeló

Top-class motor racing, including Formula 1, regularly comes to this circuit. ◉ *Apr–May • 93 571 97 71*

9 Cursa La Mercè

A 10-km (6-mile) run through Barcelona's centre. ◉ *Late Sep • 010*

10 Catalunya Rally

Top-class rally-driving in spectacular surroundings. ◉ *Oct • www.rallycatalunya.com*

For walks & bike rides in and around Barcelona **See pp58–9**

Left **Children at play, Port Olímpic beach** Right **Penguins, Parc Zoològic**

Attractions for Children

Parc d'Atraccions del Tibidabo

With its old-fashioned rides, the only surviving funfair in the city is a delight for children of all ages. The attractions include a House of Horrors, bumper cars, a ferris wheel and the Museu dels Autòmates *(see p41)*, with animatronics of all shapes and sizes. There's also a puppet show, picnic areas, playgrounds and plenty of bars and restaurants. *See p111.*

Parc Zoològic

The zoo has an enormous adventure playground where children can run wild. There are also dolphin and whale shows in one of the aquariums. Other activities for children include guided tours and workshops. The "farm" area has goats and rabbits that younger children can stroke. *See p16.*

Museu Marítim

The fantastic Maritime Museum brings the seafaring world to life with the hollering

of pirates, the report of cannons and the underwater gurgling of submarines. Well worth a look is the full-size Spanish galleon complete with sound and light effects. Set in the vast former medieval shipyards, the Drassanes, this is an absolute must for any budding sea captain. *See p81.*

L'Aquàrium

One of Europe's biggest aquariums, this underwater kingdom is made up of 21 enormous tanks brimming with nearly 400 marine species. The highlight of a visit is the Oceanari, where a walk-through glass tunnel will bring you face to face with three huge grey sharks – named Drake, Morgan and Maverick – lurking in 4.5 million litres (990,000 gallons) of water. *See p97.*

Jardins del Laberint d'Horta

The main feature of this exceptional park is the huge, hedged maze where children can live

Children, Parc Zoològic

out their *Alice in Wonderland* fantasies. Unfulfilled expectations of mad hatters are made up for by an enormous play area with a bar and terrace. The park is particularly busy on Sundays. *See p113.*

Montjuïc Cable Cars

Unlike the nerve-jangling cable-car ride across the port, these smaller, lower-altitude cable car trips are a better option if you have children with you. The ride to the Montjuïc summit also has the added appeal of the castle *(see p89)* at the top, with cannons for the kids to clamber on.

Parc de Montjuïc • Map C5 • Open Apr–Nov: 9am–10pm daily; Dec–Mar: 9am–8pm daily • Adm

La Rambla

Your shoulders will be aching from carrying the kids high above the crowds by the time you reach the end of Barcelona's main boulevard. Fire eaters, buskers, human statues decked out as Greek goddesses – you name it and it's likely to be keeping the hordes entertained on La Rambla. Put a coin in the human statue's hat and be rewarded with a sudden move, or, if you're a child, the gift of a tiny lollipop. *See pp12–13.*

City Beaches

For kids, there's more to going to the beach in Barcelona than just splashing in warm waters and frolicking in the sand.

Human statue, La Rambla

The Port Vell and Port Olímpic *platges* (beaches) offer a good choice of well-equipped play areas to keep the little ones entertained. Numerous bars and restaurants make finding refreshment easy, too. *See p97.*

Boat Trips

Barcelona's *golondrines* (see p133) make regular trips out of the port, providing a fun excursion for older children. Younger kids, however, will probably prefer paddling around in a rowing boat on the lake at the Parc de la Ciutadella (see pp16–17).

Museu d'Història de Catalunya

This child-friendly museum traces Catalonia's history through a range of dynamic, interactive exhibits. The best of these allows visitors to get dressed up as medieval knights and gallop around on wooden horses. Very popular with Catalan school groups, it's equally enjoyable for visitors. Every Saturday, the museum hosts a story hour when Catalan legends are re-enacted for children as well as other children's activities. *See p97.*

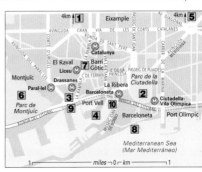

Festes de la Mercè

🔟 Catalan Folk Festivals & Traditions

1 Festes de la Mercè
Barcelona's main festival is a riotous week-long celebration in honour of La Mercè *(see p39)*. The night sky lights up with fireworks, outdoor concerts are held, and there's barely a bottle of *cava* left in the city by the festival's end. Processions and parades feature *gegants* (giant wooden figures operated by people). 🔊 *Week of 23 Sep*

Gegants, Festes de la Mercè

2 El Dia de Sant Jordi
On this spring day, Barcelona is transformed into a vibrant, open-air book and flower market. Men and women exchange presents of roses, to celebrate Sant Jordi *(see p39)* and books, in tribute to Cervantes and Shakespeare, who both died on 23 April 1616. 🔊 *23 Apr*

3 Verbena de Sant Joan
In celebration of Saint John, and the start of summer, this is Catalonian's night to play with fire and play they do, with gusto. Fireworks streak through the night sky and bonfires are set ablaze on beaches and in towns throughout the region. 🔊 *23 Jun*

4 Festa Major de Gràcia
During this week-long *festa*, (the largest party of the summer), revellers congregate in Gràcia's decorated streets. Parades, open-air concerts, fireworks and plenty of beer and cava fuel the infectious merriment. 🔊 *Mid-to late-Aug*

5 Carnaval in Sitges
The buzzing beach town of Sitges *(see p121)* explodes during Carnaval, celebrated in flamboyant fashion. Over-the-top floats parade among drag queens, lip-synching contests and a fresh-off-the-beach crowd warmed by sun and plenty of beer. 🔊 *3–4 days Feb–mid-Mar*

6 Festa de la Patum
The village of Berga (90 km/ 60 miles north of Barcelona) hosts one of Catalonia's liveliest festivals. The event gets its name from the folks who used to chant *patum* (the sound of a drum). Streets spill over with merrymakers as fireworks crackle and dwarfs, devils and dragons dance atop parade floats. 🔊 *Corpus Christi (May)*

7 Festa del Aquelarre
The small town of Cervera (100 km/62 miles west of Barcelona) erupts with parties, parades and concerts for this festival. The epicentre is C/de les Bruixes, a medieval alley that cuts through the old town. 🔊 *Last weekend Aug*

The English-language website www.spain.info has a section dedicated to Spanish festivals.

Castells

Castells is one of Catalonia's most spectacular folk traditions. Trained *castellers* stand on each other's shoulders to create a human castle – the highest tower takes the prize. The crowning moment is when a child scales the human mass to make the sign of the cross. *Castells* are often performed in Plaça Sant Jaume. ◈ *Jun*

Sardanes

"The magnificent, moving ring" is how Catalan poet Joan Maragall described the *sardana*, Catalonia's regional dance. Subdued yet intricate, it is performed to the tunes of the *cobla*, a traditional brass and woodwind band. *Sardanes* can be seen in Plaça de la Seu and Plaça Sant Jaume year round *(see p14)*.

Catalan Christmas & Cavalcada del Reis

The *Nadal* (Christmas) season begins on 1 December with the arrival of the festive artisan fairs. On 5 January is the Cavalcada dels Reis, the spectacular Three Kings Parade. In Barcelona, the kings arrive by sea and are welcomed by city officials in front of transfixed children.

Castells

Top 10 Music, Theatre & Art Festivals

Festival del Grec
Barcelona's largest music, theatre and dance festival. ◈ *late Jun–Jul* • 93 316 11 11 or 902 10 12 12

Festival del Sónar
This electronic music and multimedia festival has technology fairs and musical events. ◈ *Mid-Jun* • www.sonar.es

Festival Internacional de Jazz
Big-name and experimental live jazz. ◈ *Oct–Dec* • 93 481 70 40

Sitges International Film Festival
The foremost fantasy film festival in the world. ◈ *Early Oct* • www.cinemasitges.com

Festival de Música Antiga
Concerts of early music in the Barri Gòtic and at L'Auditori. ◈ *Apr & May* • 93 247 93 00

Clàssica als Parcs
Classical music concerts are held in the city's parks. ◈ *Jul* • 010

Festival de Guitarra
International guitar festival. ◈ *Mar–Jun* • 902 10 12 12 • www.the-project.net

Festival de Músiques del Món
Ethnic and world music acts at L'Auditori. ◈ *Oct* • 93 247 93 00

Festival de Flamenco
A week of outstanding flamenco music at the CCCB in the Raval. ◈ *Late May* • 93 443 43 46

Festival de Música
The Spanish village of Llívia, just over the French border, presents choral groups and orchestras from around the world. ◈ *Llívia* • Aug & Dec • 972 89 63 13

Left **Teatre Grec** Right **Gran Teatre del Liceu**

🔟 Performing Arts & Music Venues

1 Gran Teatre del Liceu
Phoenix-like, the Liceu has risen from the ashes of two devastating fires since its inauguration in 1847. Now one of the greatest opera houses in Europe, it has an innovative programme and is famed for performances by home-grown talent, including one of the "three tenors" José Carreras, as well as Montserrat Caballé. ◎ *La Rambla • Map L4 • 93 485 99 13 • Guided tour 10am daily • Adm • DA*

2 Palau Sant Jordi
The star of the Olympic buildings, this stadium is normally home to Barcelona's basketball team *(see p61)*. It doubles up as the city's main arena for macroconcerts, which have included Madonna and U2. *See p90.* ◎ *Box office: 93 426 20 89 • Open for visits 10am–6pm (8pm Jul & Aug) Sat & Sun • Free • DA*

3 Teatre Grec
The most magical and enigmatic of all Barcelona's venues, this open-air amphitheatre, set in thick, verdant forest, makes an incredible setting for ballet, music or theatre. Only used for shows during the summer arts Festival del Grec, the gardens are open all year to visitors. *See p90.* ◎ *Box office: 93 301 77 75 • Open for visits 10am–dusk daily • Free*

4 Palau de la Música Catalana
Domenèch i Montaner's epic *Modernista* gem regularly serves up the best in jazz and classical music. It has lost some of its prestige to the Auditori, but it still hosts the annual guitar festival and attracts many visiting world music artists. *See pp26–7.*

5 Auditori de Barcelona
Located near the Teatre Nacional, this large auditorium is home to the Orquestra Simfònica de Barcelona. Acoustics and visibility are excellent and, in addition to classical music, it hosts regular jazz concerts. ◎ *C/Lepant 150 • Map G1 • 93 247 93 00 • DA*

Concert, Palau de la Música Catalana

6 Harlem Jazz Club
This small, intimate venue is one of the longest surviving clubs for alternative and lesser-known jazz and blues troupes. Free entrance if you buy a drink. *See p77.* ◎ *93 310 07 55*

For Catalan speakers, the Teatre Nacional de Catalunya (93 306 57 00) is a fine showcase for Catalan drama.

7 Mercat de les Flors

This is the venue of choice for performance theatre groups, such as La Fura dels Baus and Comediants, whose incredible mixture of circus and drama is easily accessible to non-Catalan speakers. ◈ C/Lleida 59 • Map B4 • 93 426 18 75 • www.mercatflors.org

8 Club Apolo

An old dance hall, with velvet covered balconies and panelled bars, this place has reinvented itself as one of the city's leading nightclubs. It attracts the latest in live techno and dance music. ◈ C/Nou de la Rambla 113 • Map K4 • 93 441 40 01 • www.sala-apolo.com

Harlem Jazz Club

9 La Paloma

Another reformed dance hall, La Paloma competes with Club Apolo for the latest rising stars in pop and dance music. It still has traditional tea dances with live orchestras, but this is strictly ballroom: two step, waltz, salsa, rumba and lots of cha cha cha. ◈ C/Tigre 27 • Map J1 • 93 301 6897 • Closed for renovation until 2008 • www.lapaloma-bcn.com

10 Club Fellini

This club offers three different spaces: the Mirrors Lounge, with chic house music, the Bad Room, with electronic sessions, and the Red Room, the perfect space for flirting. ◈ La Rambla 27 • Map L5 • 93 272 49 80 • www.clubfellini.com

Top 10 Versión Original Cinemas

1 Verdi

One of the original VO cinemas, with five different screens. ◈ C/Verdi 32 • Map B2 • 93 238 79 90

2 Icària Yelmo Cineplex

An incredible 15 screens all showing original version films. ◈ C/Salvador Espriu 61 • Map H5 • 90 222 09 22

3 Casablanca

An old style, two-screen, cinema, which has retained its character. ◈ Pg de Gràcia 115 • Map E2 • 93 218 43 45

4 Boliche

A four-screen cinema showing mainly European films. ◈ Av Diagonal 508 • Map E1 • 93 218 17 88

5 Méliès Cinemes

Two-screened repertory cinema. ◈ C/Villarroel 102 • Map J1 • 93 451 00 51

6 Renoir-Les Corts

Multi-screened cinema with lots of Spanish and English films. ◈ C/Eugeni d'Ors 12 • Map A2 • 90 222 16 22

7 Verdi Park

Four-screen version of the original Verdi. ◈ C/Torrijos 49 • Map F1 • 93 238 79 90

8 Renoir Floridablanca

A multiplex that shows films from around the world. ◈ Floridablanca 135 • Map C3 • 90 222 16 22

9 Maldà

A small new cinema showing independent and Bollywood movies. ◈ C/del Pi 5 • Map M3 • 639 749 427

10 Filmoteca

The Catalan government's repertory cinema runs three VO shows daily. ◈ Av Sarrià 31–33 • Map D1 • 93 410 75 90 • Closed Aug

Barcelona's many versió original (original version) cinemas provide plenty of options for non-Catalan-speaking film aficionados.

AROUND TOWN

BARCELONA'S TOP 10

Left **Museu d'Història de la Ciutat** Right **Saló de Cent, Ajuntament**

Barri Gòtic & La Ribera

THOUGH HARD TO IMAGINE TODAY, *there was a timewhen Barcelona was just a small Roman village (named Barcino) encircled by protective stone walls. Over the centuries, the village grew, culminating in a building boom in the 14th and 15th centuries. The Barri Gòtic (Gothic Quarter), a beautifully preserved neighbourhood of Gothic buildings, medieval places (squares) and atmospheric alleys, exists today as a splendid reminder of Barcelona's medieval heyday. The web of ancient, treasure-filled streets in this compact area is best explored by aimless wandering. The barrio's centrepiece – and its religious and social heart – is the 13th–century Cathedral and surrounding complex of period buildings. Nearby, the stately Plaça del Rei (see p36) is ringed by some of the best preserved medieval buildings in the area. Extending*

east of the Barri Gòtic is *the ancient barrio of La Ribera, which includes El Born (see p72). Here, the lovely Carrer Montcada is lined with medieval palaces – five of which house the must-see Museu Picasso.*

Roman Arch, Carrer Paradis

📑 Sights

1. Barcelona Cathedral
2. Museu Picasso
3. Palau de la Música Catalana
4. Plaça de Sant Jaume
5. Conjunt Monumental de la Plaça del Rei
6. Plaça Reial
7. Museu Frederic Marès
8. Església de Santa Maria del Mar
9. Museu Tèxtil i d'Indumentèria
10. Museu Barbier–Mueller d'Art Precolombí

For sights & attractions on La Rambla See pp12–13

1 Barcelona Cathedral

Soaring over the Barri Gòtic is Barcelona's mighty Cathedral dating from 1298. See pp14–15.

2 Museu Picasso

Discover the youthful repertoire of one of the 20th-century's most revered artists. See pp24–5.

3 Palau de la Música Catalana

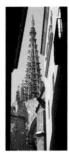

Cathedral spire

The city's most prestigious concert hall is a monument to both la musica Catalana and to Modernisme. See pp26–7.

4 Plaça de Sant Jaume

The site of the Plaça de Sant Jaume (see p36) was once the nucleus of Roman Barcino. With these roots, it seems fitting that the square has become home to Barcelona's two most important government buildings: the Palau de la Generalitat (seat of the Catalan government) and the Ajuntament (city hall). Look for the detailed carved relief of Sant Jordi, Catalonia's patron saint, on the 15th-century Generalitat façade. Within is the lovely 15th-century Capella de Sant Jordi (see p39), designed by architect Marc Safont. A highlight of the Gothic Ajuntament is the lavish red-and-gold Saló de Cent, where the Council of One Hundred ruled the city from 1372 to 1714. Also of note is the Pati dels Tarongers, a graceful patio with orange trees. *Palau de la Generalitat • Pl de Sant Jaume • Map M4 • Open 10:30am–1:30pm 2nd & 4th Sun of month for guided tours • Free* *Ajuntament • Pl de Sant Jaume • Map M4 • Open 10am–1:30pm Sun for guided tours • Free*

5 Conjunt Monumental de la Plaça del Rei

In the heart of the Barri Gòtic is the beautifully preserved, medieval Plaça del Rei (see p36), presided over by the 13th- to 14th-century Palau Reial (royal palace). The impressive palace complex includes the Saló del Tinell, a massive hall crowned by Gothic arches, where Ferdinand and Isabel welcomed Columbus after his 1492 voyage to the Americas. The medieval Capella de Santa Àgata has a beautiful 15th-century altarpiece by Jaume Huguet. A visit to the Museu d'Història de la Ciutat gives access to the Palau Reial and to one of the largest underground excavations of Roman ruins on display in Europe. *Pl del Rei • Map M4 • Open 10am–8pm Tue–Sat, 10am–3pm Sun (Oct–May: closes 2–4pm) • Adm • DA*

Left **Italianate façade, Palau de la Generalitat** Right **Mosaic pillar, Palau de la Música Catalana**

For more on Barri Gòtic squares See pp36–7

El Born

If you're hankering for a proper martini or perhaps some alternative jazz, then look no further than El Born, a musty-turned-hip neighbourhood, which was "reborn" several years ago. Students and artists moved in, attracted by cheap rents and airy warehouses, fostering an arty vibe that now blends in with the area's old–time aura. Experimental design shops share the narrow streets with traditional, balconied buildings strung with laundry. The bustling Passeig de Born, lined with bars and cafés, leads onto the lively Plaça Comercial, where the cavernous Born Market (in operation 1870–1970) is now being converted into a cultural centre and exhibition space (to open in 2008).

Plaça Reial (1850s)

Plaça Reial

Late 19th-century elegance meets sangria-swilling café society in the arcaded Plaça Reial, one of Barcelona's most emblematic and entertaining squares. The *plaça* is planted with towering palm trees and encircled by stately, 19th-century buildings. The *Modernista* lampposts were designed by a young Gaudí in 1879. At the square's centre is a wrought-iron fountain representing the Three Graces. The square is the best place to start a big night out, with a cluster of restaurants, bars and cafés that draw the hoi polloi – including all sorts of shady pickpockets. ✪ *Map L4*

Medieval arch, Museu Frederic Marès

Museu Frederic Marès

A fascinating shrine to objects large and small, this museum houses the life collection of wealthy Catalan sculptor Frederic Marès. No mere hobby collector, the astute (and obsessive) Marès amassed holdings that a modern museum curator would die for. Among them, an impressive array of religious icons and statues – dating from Roman times to the present – and the spectacular "Museu Sentimental", which displays anything from ancient watches to fans and dolls. Also worth a visit is the inviting Cafè d'Estiu *(see p78)* on the museum's sun-dappled patio. ✪ *Pl de Sant Iu 5–6 • Map N3 • Open 10am–7pm Tue–Sat, 10am–3pm Sun • Adm €3 (con €1.50); free Wed pm & 1st Sun of month*

Església de Santa Maria del Mar

The spacious, breathtaking interior of this 14th–century church, designed by architect Berenguer de Montagut, is the city's premier example of the austere Catalan Gothic style. The church is dedicated to Saint Mary of the Sea, the patron saint of sailors, and an ancient model ship hangs near one of the statues of the Virgin. Dubbed "the people's church", this is the city's most popular spot for exchanging wedding vows. ✪ *Pl de Santa Maria 1 • Map P5 • Open 9am–1:30pm & 4:30–8pm*

 Share your travel recommendations on traveldk.com

Centre del Disseny

Housed in a pair of adjoining medieval palaces, the Centre del Disseny (Design Centre) combines activities from different areas: architecture, graphic and communications design, product design and fashion design. The small but ultra-cool museum shop sells funky clothes, accessories and design collectables, while the café beckons with outdoor tables in a shady courtyard. In 2011 the collection will be moved to a new museum currently under construction in Plaça de les Glories. ◈ *C/Montcada 12–14 • Map P4 • Open 10am–6pm Tue–Sat, 10am–3pm Sun • Adm • DA*

Museu Barbier-Mueller d'Art Precolombè

Pre-Columbian art and artifacts, spanning 3,000 years, are exhibited in the 16th-century Palau Nadal. Sculpture, ceramics and detailed gold and silver pieces represent the rich artistic traditions of the Aztecs, Mayans and Incas. Temporary exhibits explore the diversity of these civilizations. ◈ *C/Montcada 12–14 • Map P4 • Open 11am–7pm Tue–Fri, 10am–7pm Sat, (3pm Sun) • Adm; free 1st Sun of month • DA*

Interior, Església de Santa Maria del Mar

Roman Barcelona

Morning

Starting at the Jaume I metro, enter the ancient walled city of Barcino on C/Llibreteria, once the main road to and from Rome. Head right up C/Veguer to **Plaça del Rei** *(see p36)* and descend into a fascinating underground web of Roman walls and waterways via the **Museu d'Història de la Ciutat** *(see p71)*. Also visible here are the remains of a 2nd-century workshop and an ancient bodega, a source of much Roman merrymaking. Back above ground, pause for a *cafè sol* at the terrace of **Café–Bar L'Antiquari** *(see p78)* and bask in Barcelona's Gothic glory days. Stroll towards the Cathedral's spires along C/de la Pietat. Turn right onto C/Bisbe, once a Roman thoroughfare, then right again on Av de la Catedral to visit the **Pia Almoina** *(see p15)*, where you can view a section of the Roman aqueduct and ride a glass elevator past Roman wall remains. Backtrack to Plaça Nova, once the Roman gateway to Barcino, cross the *plaça* and continue along C/Arcs.

Afternoon

Stop for lunch at the **Reial Cercle Artèstic**, a late 19th-century artists' society. Ignore the "members only" sign; the restaurant is open to the public, and its tranquil balcony terrace provides a welcome breather from the crowds far below. After lunch, head up Av del Portal de l'Àngel and turn left onto C/Canuda to **Plaça de la Vila de Madrid** *(see p37)*. The square is a fitting end to your Roman ramble, for here are the necropolis remains, where Romans came to rest.

For more museums **See pp40–41**

Left **Carrer del Bisbe** Centre **Església de Sant Just i Sant Pastor** Right **Plaça de Sant Felip Neri**

Best of the Rest

Carrer del Bisbe
Medieval Carrer del Bisbe is flanked by the Gothic Cases dels Canonges (House of Canons) and the Palau de la Generalitat *(see p71)*. Connecting the two is an eye-catching Neo-Gothic arched stone bridge (1928). ◈ *Map M3*

Carrer de Santa Llúcia
At weekends, amateur opera singers perform on this medieval street, home to the Casa de l'Ardiaca *(see p15)*, which has a ravishing little patio. ◈ *Map M3*

El Call
El Call was home to one of Spain's largest Jewish communities until their expulsion in the 15th century. The dark streets of this ghetto are so narrow it is said you can tie a handkerchief across their width. ◈ *Map M4*

Carrer Montcada
The "palace row" of La Ribera is lined with Gothic architectural gems, including the 15th-century Palau Aguilar, home to the Museu Picasso *(see pp24–5)*, and the 17th-century Palau Dalmases with its Gothic chapel. ◈ *Map P4*

Plaça de Ramon Berenguer el Gran
This square boasts one of the largest intact sections of Barcelona's Roman walls. ◈ *Map N3*

Carrer Regomir & Carrer del Correu Vell
You'll find splendid Roman remains on Carrer Regomir, most notably within the medieval Pati Llimona. Two Roman towers are revealed on nearby Carrer del Correu Vell, and there are Roman walls on the leafy Plaça Traginers. ◈ *Map M5*

Plaça de Sant Felip Neri
Sunlight filters through tall trees in this hidden oasis of calm. The *plaça* is home to the Museu del Calçat *(see p41)*. ◈ *Map M3*

Carrer Petritxol
This well-maintained medieval street is lined with traditional *granges* and *xocolateries* (confectionary cafés). Also here is the famous Sala Parés art gallery, founded in 1877, which once exhibited Picasso, Casas and other Catalan contemporaries. ◈ *Map L3*

Església de Sant Just i Sant Pastor
This picturesque Gothic church (1342) has sculptures inside that date back to the 9th century. ◈ *Map M4*

Església de Santa Anna
Mere paces from La Rambla is the unexpected tranquillity of this Romanesque church, with a leafy, 15th-century, Gothic cloister. ◈ *Map M2*

For more Barcelona squares **See pp36–7**

Left **Escribà Confiteria i Fleca** Centre **Accessories, El Mercadillo** Right **Exterior, El Mercadillo**

🔟 Shops: Gifts, Garments & Goodies

Escribà Confiteria i Fleca
If the glistening pastries and towering chocolate creations aren't enough of a lure, then the *Modernista* store-front certainly is. Buy goodies to go, or enjoy them on the spot in the small café. ◈ *La Rambla 83 • Map L3*

Art Escudellers
This warehouse-sized store has a vast array of colourful handmade ceramics from all over Spain. Take your pick from a superb selection of Spanish wines and cured hams in the wine cellar. ◈ *C/Escudellers 23–25 • Map L5*

4rt Montfalcón
Housed in the 15th-century Palau Castanyer, this enormous shop stocks posters, photos, oil paintings, souvenirs and prints of works by well-known Spanish artists. ◈ *C/Boters 4 • Map M3*

Atalanta Manufactura
This shop's delicate, handpainted silks are created in an on-site workshop. Unusual designs include a Klimt-inspired, gilded silk. ◈ *Pg del Born 10 • Map P5*

La Manual Alpargatera
What do the Pope, Jack Nicholson and legions of *Barcelonins* have in common? They buy their espadrilles (*alpargatas*) here. ◈ *C/Avinyó 7 • Map M4*

Casa Colomina
Sink your teeth into *torró*, the Spanish nougat-and-almond speciality. Casa Colomina, established in 1908, offers a tantalizing array. ◈ *C/Portaferrissa 8 • Map L3*

Cereria Subirà
Founded in 1761, this is Barcelona's oldest shop. Today you'll find it crammed with every kind of candle imaginable. ◈ *Baixada Llibreteria 7 • Map N4*

L'Arca de l'Àvia
Amazing antique clothing from flapper dresses to boned corsets, silk shawls, puff sleeved shirts and pin-tucked shirt fronts. There's also a selection of antique dolls and fans. ◈ *C/Banys Nous 20 • Map M3*

Guantería Alonso
This long-established shop is still the place to visit if you are looking for colourful handpainted fans, handmade gloves, delicately embroidered shawls, ornamental combs and other traditional Spanish accessories. ◈ *C/Santa Anna 27 • Map M2*

El Mercadillo
A neon-lit mini-mall, with vintage clothes, records and trendy accessories, all housed in a stately 18th-century palace. ◈ *C/Portaferrissa 17 • Map M3*

Left **La Vinya del Senyor** Right **Schilling**

🔟 Cocktail & Conversation Spots

1 Schilling
Fronted by large windows overlooking the throngs on Carrer Ferran, this spacious bar draws a sociable mix of both visitors and locals. ⊗ *C/Ferran 23 • Map M4*

2 Bar L'Ascensor
An old-fashioned, dark-wood *ascensor* (elevator) serves as the entrance to this dimly-lit, convivial bar frequented by a cocktail-swilling crowd. ⊗ *C/Bellafila 3 • Map M4*

3 Espai Barroc
Filling the gorgeous courtyard of the 17th-century Palau Dalmases is this sumptuously decorated "Baroque Space". Live opera and classical music are often featured in the evenings, but drinks are pricey. ⊗ *C/Montcada 20 • Map P4 • Closed Mon*

4 Ginger
An elegant bar that serves fine wines, champagne, cava, cocktails and a variety of original tapas to a glamorous crowd. ⊗ *Palma de Sant Just 1 • Map N4 • Closed Mon, Sun*

5 Glaciar
Occupying a prime corner of Plaça Reial, this atmospheric café-bar brings in all types. Grab a spot on the terrace with a front-row view of the *plaça* activities. ⊗ *Pl Reial 3 • Map L4*

6 Padam
Tucked into an alley off Carrer Ferran, this small, dimly lit, old-style bar plays tunes by Edith Piaf (including the famous *Padam*, of course) and her contemporaries. ⊗ *C/Ràuric 9 • Map L4 • Closed Sun*

7 La Vinya del Senyor
A classy, yet cosy, bar attracting wine lovers from all over the city, who come to sample a rich array of Spanish and international varieties in the company of other wine aficionados. ⊗ *Pl Santa Maria 5 • Map N5 • Closed Mon*

8 Suborn
Start your evening at this busy El Born café-restaurant. Or end it here as night descends and it transforms into a bar-club with DJ-spun house and techno. ⊗ *C/Ribera 18 • Map P5 • Closed Mon*

9 Gimlet
The original cocktail bar in El Born, the intimate, 1950s-style Gimlet pours nice (read: potent) cocktails to a local clientele. ⊗ *C/Rec 24 • Map P4 • Closed Sun*

10 Mudanzas
This long-time favourite hang-out has circular marble tables, black-and-white tiled floors and an informal, "everyone's welcome" vibe. ⊗ *C/Vidrieria 15 • Map P5*

Unless otherwise stated, bars, clubs & music venues are open daily.

Left **Sidecar Factory Club** Right **Bar, Fonfone**

🔟 Clubs & Music Venues

1 Jamboree
This Barri Gòtic institution has live jazz every night (11pm–1am). It then evolves into a dance club, with DJs spinning everything from hip-hop to R&B and salsa. ◈ Pl Reial 17 • Map L4 • Adm

2 Dot Light Club
Urbanites flock to this popular nightspot to groove to anything from Mambo Moves to Loungin' chill-out tunes. ◈ C/Nou de Sant Francesc 7 • Map L5 • Closed Mon

3 Club 13
One of the most glamorous places in the Old Town, Club 13 has a restaurant and terrace on the ground floor, and a nightclub in the basement, which is decorated in gold and red velvet. ◈ Plaza Reial 13 • Map L4

4 Harlem Jazz Club
Dark and smoky, this kick-back jazz haunt features a choice line-up of jazz and blues, flamenco fusion, reggae and African music. ◈ Comtessa de Sobradiel 8 • Map M5 • Usually free • Closed Mon

5 Sala Monasterio
Head to this venue of brick walls and arches for excellent live music, ranging from flamenco and chanson, to rock and blues (Thu). ◈ Pg Isabel II 4 • Map N5 • Adm • Closed Mon–Wed

6 Karma
The hippie origins and 1970s glamour at this club are as popular as ever. ◈ Pl Reial 10 • Map L4 • Adm • Closed Mon

7 Magic
Live music is played here at weekends by new, up-and-coming Spanish bands. After the show, the dancing goes on until 5:30am. ◈ Pg Picasso 40 • Map P4 • Adm • Closed Sun–Wed

8 Fonfone
A contemporary club awash with backlit geometric shapes. Different dance sounds every night, from fusion jazz to house music. ◈ C/Escudellers 24 • Map L5

9 Al Limón Negro
The eclectic "Black Lemon" restaurant-club features ethnic and world music concerts, performance art and occasional art exhibitions. ◈ C/Escudellers Blancs 3 • Map L4 • Closed Mon

10 Sidecar Factory Club
Barcelona's music scene is like a motorbike to which Sidecar is inseparably bound. They say the American 6th fleet once hired the whole venue and made merry. Music, theatre, cabaret, video and good food can all be found. ◈ Pl Reial 7 • Map L4 • Adm • Closed Sun

Catalunya
Liceu
Jaume I
Drassanes
Estació de França

Around Town – Barri Gòtic & La Ribera

For Barcelona's best nightlife **See pp46–7**

Left **Terrace, Cafè-Bar L'Antiquari** Centre **Ice cream, Cafè d'Estiu** Right **Cafè-Bar Jardín**

🔟 Cafés & Light Eats

Cafè d'Estiu
Tucked away on the patio of the Museu Frederic Marès *(see p72)* is this alluring, sun-strewn terrace café, replete with stone pillars, climbing ivy and orange trees. ◈ *Pl de Sant Lluc 5–6 • Map N3 • Closed Mon & Oct–Mar • DA*

Cafè-Bar Jardín
This lovely outdoor café, hidden upstairs at El Mercadillo *(see p75)*, is shaded by trees and vine-covered walls. ◈ *C/Porta-ferrisa 17 • Map M3 • Closed Sun*

Cafè-Bar L'Antiquari
In summer, bask in the old town's medieval atmosphere at the Plaça del Rei terrace. By night, sip Rioja in the intimate, rustic basement bodega.
◈ *C/Veguer 13 • Map N4*

Cafè-Bar del Pi
The Església de Santa Maria del Pi casts a shadow over this café's terrace. And for when you're in that kick-back-and-do-nothing mode, street artists keep you entertained. ◈ *Pl Santa Josep Oriol 1 • Map M4 • Closed Tue*

Tetería Salterio
Sit back and relax with tea and sweet Arab cakes. Do not miss the Sado, an Oriental style pizza with a variety of fillings. ◈ *Sant Domenec del Call 4 • Map M4*

Cava Universal
At the foot of the Columbus statue *(see p12)*, this long-time café is a choice spot to soak up the rays, knock back a beer and people-watch. ◈ *Pl Portal de la Pau 4 • Map L6 • DA*

Café del Born
Plaça Comercial is dotted with cafés, including the laid-back Café del Born, which evolves into an amiable bar as night descends. ◈ *Pl Comercial 10 • Map P4*

Caelum
Uptairs sells honey, pre-serves and other foods made in convents and monasteries all over Spain. Downstairs you can sample all the delicacies in a cosy café on the site of a 15th century baths.
◈ *C/Palla 8 • Map M3 • Closed Sun*

Venus Delicatessen
Colourful and inviting, this café-restaurant serves great cof-fee and tea as well as plenty of fresh fare, including innovative salads such as "Erotica", with asparagus, tuna and tomato.
◈ *C/Avinyó 25 • Map M5 • Closed Sun*

Xocoa
This family-run *xocolateria* has long been serving up decadent desserts and baked goodies, such as fig ravioli with peach ice-cream. ◈ *C/Petritxol 11 • Map L3*

For more cafés in the Barri Gòtic **See pp42–3**

Price Categories

For a three-course meal for one with half a bottle of wine (or equivalent meal), taxes and extra charges.

€	up to €10
€€	€10–20
€€€	€20–30
€€€€	over €30

Left **Outdoor terrace, Taxidermista**

TOP 10 Restaurants & Tapas Bars

1 Agut d'Avignon
A French-Catalan restaurant housed in a 17th-century building. Home-style cuisine with a twist includes duck with figs and goose flavoured with pears. ® C/Trinitat 3 • Map M4 • 93 302 60 34 • €€€€

2 Cal Pep
Taste the tantalizing tapas, including the finest cured hams, at this established eatery. ® Pl de les Olles 8 • Map P5 • 93 310 79 61 • Closed Sun & Mon lunch • €€€€

3 Cafè de l'Acadèmia
Superb Catalan cuisine and top-notch desserts are served at this restaurant in an 18th-century building. ® C/Lledó 1 • Map N4 • 93 315 00 26 • Closed Sat & Sun • €€€

4 Taxidermista
Dine under the Plaça Reial's arches at this stylish restaurant in a former taxidermist's shop. The first-rate menu offers the likes of white tuna with capers. ® Pl Reial 8 • Map L4 • 93 412 45 36 • Closed Mon • DA • €€€

5 Senyor Parellada
Excellent Catalan cuisine, including speciality bacalao (cod) and butifarra (sausage), is the deal at this elegant restaurant. ® C/Argenteria 37 • Map N4 • 93 310 50 94 • €€€

6 Agut
For over 75 years, this friendly, family restaurant has been delighting patrons with excellent Catalan cuisine at decent prices. ® C/Gignàs 16 • Map M5 • 93 315 17 09 • Closed Sun eve & Mon • €€€€

7 Txakolin
At the large bar enjoy great Basque-style pinchos (tapas), from cured ham to creamy crab salad. The restaurant serves superb Basque fish and meat dishes. ® C/Marqués de l'Argentera 19 • Map P5 • 93 268 1781 • Closed Sun eve & Mon • €€€€

8 Salero
The "Salt Cellar" has an all-white interior offset by flickering candles. An innovative menu features Mediterranean-Asian fusion cuisine. ® C/Rec 60 • Map P5 • 93 319 80 22 • Closed Sun • €€€

9 El Xampanyet
A boisterous tapas bar serving champagne, pitchers of cider and generous portions of tapas. ® C/Montcada 22 • Map P4 • 93 319 70 03 • Closed Sun eve, & Mon • €€

10 Govinda
This soothing eatery offers vegetarian Indian main dishes and delectable desserts, but no alcohol. ® Pl Vila de Madrid 4–5 • Map M2 • 93 318 77 29 • Closed Sun eve & Mon eve • DA • €€€

Unless otherwise stated, all restaurants accept credit cards.
For tips on dining and standard opening hours See p138

Left **Plaça de Joan Coromines** Right **Columns, Església de Sant Pau del Camp**

El Raval

THE SLEEK, SHINY, WHITE WALLS of the Museu d'Art Contemporani (MACBA) juxtapose the decrepit, ramshackle tenement buildings; Asian grocery stores sell herbs and spices next to what were once the most decadent brothels in Europe; and smoky, decades-old bars share dark, narrow streets with high-ceilinged art galleries showcasing video installations. The old-town barrio of El Raval is a traditional working-class neighbourhood in flux. Over the last decade it has been undergoing an enthusiastic urban renewal, led by the arrival of the MACBA. The barrio now even has its very own Rambla, a new pedestrian street called La Rambla del Raval. Not surprisingly, all of this has sparked a real-estate boom, with renovated old-fashioned flats now commanding top-tier prices and acting as a magnet to the city's young, savvy crowd.

Stained-glass window, Museu Marítim

🔟 Sights

1. Museu d'Art Contemporani
2. Centre de Cultura Contemporània & Foment de les Arts Decoratives
3. Museu Marítim
4. Palau Güell
5. La Rambla del Raval
6. Carrer Nou de la Rambla
7. Carrers Tallers & Riera Baixa
8. Barri Xinès
9. Antic Hospital de la Santa Creu
10. Església de Sant Pau del Camp

For sights & attractions on La Rambla **See pp12–13**

1 Museu d'Art Contemporani

An eclectic array of work by big-name Spanish and international contemporary artists is gathered in the city's contemporary art museum. Excellent temporary exhibitions feature everything from mixed media to sculpture and photography. *See pp28–9.*

Central salon cupola, Palau Güell

2 Centre de Cultura Contemporània & Foment de les Arts Decoratives

Housed in the 18th-century Casa de la Caritat, the CCCB is a focal point for the city's thriving contemporary arts scene. It hosts innovative art exhibitions, lectures, film screenings and more, including multimedia and technology fairs during the popular Festival del Sònar *(see p65)*. A medieval courtyard is dazzlingly offset by a massive, angled glass wall, which has been cunningly designed to reflect the city's skyline. Nearby, Foment de les Arts Decoratives *(see p84)* is an umbrella organization of art and design groups, founded in 1903 and housed in the restored, Gothic-style, 16th-century Convent dels Àngels. Here you'll find exhibits, lectures and debates, and a smashing café-restaurant. *See pp28–9.*

3 Museu Marítim

Barcelona's mighty seafaring legacy comes to life at this impressive museum housed in the vast, 13th-century Drassanes Reials (Royal Shipyards). Wander beneath looming Gothic arches and relive Barcelona's maritime history through exhibits of model ships, old maps and figureheads. A highlight is the full-scale replica of the Royal, the ship commanded by Don Juan of Austria during the Battle of Lepanto in 1571. Entrance also includes a visit to the Pailebot *Santa Eulàlia (see p98)*, a restored wooden sailing ship dating from 1918. ◈ *Av de les Drassanes • Map K6 • Open 10am–8pm daily • Adm €6.50 (con €5.20)*

4 Palau Güell

For an artist, a wealthy patron spells survival. The luck of young Gaudí turned when count Eusebi Güell recognized his talents. In 1886, Güell commissioned Gaudí to build a mansion that would set the count apart from his wealthy neighbours. The result is the Palau Güell, one of Gaudí's earliest works. An imposing façade gives way to an elaborate interior of lavish pillars and carved wooden ceilings, while the rooftop has a melange of mosaic chimneys. ◈ *C/Nou de la Rambla 3–5 • Map L4 • Open for guided visits every 15 mins 10am–6:15pm Mon–Sat • Adm €3 • Closed for renovations until the end of 2007*

Puzzle table, Museu d'Art Contemporani

For more on Antoni Gaudí **See p11**

La Rambla del Raval

This palm tree-lined, pedestrian walkway is the latest attempt by city planners to spark a similar social environment to that of the city's famed La Rambla (see pp12–13). So far it is off to a creaking start, with barely a fraction of the crowds that ply the original Rambla. Its advocates, however, are quick to point out that La Rambla del Raval is far better than the two dark, run-down streets that formerly existed here. New shops, bars and cafés mean it could well rival its cousin in years to come. ◉ Map K4

Carrer Nou de la Rambla

In the first half of the 19th century, El Raval's main street was a notorious strip of cabarets, brothels and other nocturnal dens. Today it still bustles with transactions, but of a different sort. Frayed-at-the-edge local eateries, ethnic grocery stores, and discount clothing and shoe shops dot the street. And nightspots, such as the atmospheric London Bar (see p86), which have conserved their age-old identity and fixtures, lure partying visitors. ◉ Map J5

Carrers Tallers & Riera Baixa

Looking for bootleg CDs of Madonna's European tour? Or

Shoppers, Carrer Taller

vintage blue-and-white French navy tops once favoured by the likes of Picasso? Dotting Carrers Tallers and Riera Baixa, in the heart of El Raval, is a host of vintage music and clothing shops selling everything from vinyl to the latest CDs, original Hawaiian shirts and Dickies workwear. On Saturdays from 11am to 9pm, Carrer Riera Baixa hosts its own market, when the stores display their wares on the street. ◉ Map L1 & K3

Barri Xinès

The first thing locals will say when you ask about the Barri Xinès is that it no longer exists; the second is that the name has no real connection with the Chinese (Xinès). Both statements are true. This barrio, unfolding south from Carrer Sant Pau towards Drassanes, was once one of Europe's most infamous neighbourhoods, inhabited by the poor and working-class and rife with prostitutes, pimps, strippers and drug dealers. Today, due to enthusiastic clean-up efforts, mere vestiges remain of the barrio's

Record shop, Carrer Tallers

previous life (though some alleys still hint at illicit activity). As for the name, the area has nothing to do with the Chinese, but was named in the barrio's early-1900s heyday as a general reference to its large immigrant population. Today you can browse in cheap thrift shops and small grocery stores by day and bar-hop your way through the area by night. ⚲ Map K4

Antic Hospital de la Santa Creu

A rich reminder of the neighbourhoods' medieval past is this Gothic hospital complex (1401), which is today home to educational and cultural organizations. Within, you can wander a pleasant garden surrounded by Gothic pillars. ⚲ Entrances on C/Carme & C/Hospital 56 • Map K3 • 9am–8pm daily • Free

Cloister, Església de Sant Pau del Camp

Església de Sant Pau del Camp

Deep in the heart of El Raval is this Romanesque church, one of the oldest in Barcelona. Originally founded as a Benedictine monastery in the 9th century and subsequently rebuilt, this ancient church reveals a peaceful, 12th-century cloister. ⚲ C/Sant Pau 101 • Map J4 • Open 5–8pm Mon; 10am–1:30pm, 5–8pm Tue–Fri; 10am–1:30pm Sat • Adm €1.50

A Ramble in El Raval

Morning

🕐 Start your ramble mid-morning by perusing the innovative temporary art exhibits at the **CCCB** (see p81). Here the two world's have meshed harmoniously. The eye-catching blend of old-meets-new in this cutting-edge art space provides a fitting introduction to El Raval's new identity. Head south along C/Montalegre to the Plaça dels Àngels. Sip a coffee beneath the Gothic arches of the restored Convent dels Àngels, which houses the café-restaurant and art and design exhibition rooms of **Foment de les Arts Decoratives** (see p81). Round off your art amble with a trip down nearby C/Doctor Dou, which is speckled with commercial art galleries. If you're looking for contemporary art to jazz up your home, pop into **Ego** or **Cotthem Gallery** (see p84).

Afternoon

From here, it's a short saunter to **Mercat de La Boqueria** (see p12). Walk along C/Carme, turn left onto C/Jerusalem, and go into the back entrance of this cavernous market. Make a beeline for El Quim de La Boqueria (stall 584–585) where you can pull up a stool and dig into fresh fare from baby prawns drizzled in olive oil and garlic to steamed mussels. After, head to the medieval gardens of the **Antic Hospital de la Santa Creu**, off C/Hospital, and take in the Gothic ambience of pillared arcades and courtyards. Then, get to **Marsella** (see p86) and kick-start the evening with an absinthe before making for **London Bar** (see p86), where live music awaits.

Left **Contemporary art display** Right **Window, Foment de les Arts Decoratives**

🔟 Galleries & Design Shops

Galeria dels Àngels
Emerging and established contemporary artists from home and abroad are shown at this cutting-edge photography, painting and sculpture gallery. ◈ C/Àngels 16 • Map K2 • Closed Sun & Mon

KBB – Kültur Büro Barcelona
Contemporary art and culture by national and international artists is on display. KBB is also used as a platform for interactive projects discussing topical issues. ◈ Joaquín Costa 24, 4th floor • Map K2 • Open 4–8pm Wed–Sat

Espai Ras
Exhibits at this architecture and design gallery and bookstore include architectural models, video installations and graphic design. ◈ C/Doctor Dou 10 • Map L2 • Closed Sun & Mon

Bagués Joieria
Iconic Barcelona jeweller since 1839 with an international reputation. Each piece is hand-made using traditional methods. ◈ La Rambla 105 • Map L3 • Closed Sun

Cotthem Gallery
This long-established gallery exhibits one of the finest line-ups of international contemporary artists in Barcelona. ◈ C/Doctor Dou 15 • Map L2 • Closed Sun & Mon

La Capella
As well as contemporary art, this gallery boasts the R. Punt space, where you can relax and read dozens of art magazines. ◈ C/Hospital 56 • Map K3 • Open noon–2pm & 4–8pm Tue–Sat, 11am–2pm Sun

Foment de les Arts Decoratives (FAD)
Check out the ongoing exhibitions hosted by FAD, a century-old arts, crafts and design organization. Also here is Items d'Ho, a quirky shop selling creative furnishings, bags and jewellery. ◈ Pl Àngels 5–6 • Map K2 • Closed Sun

La Xina A.R.T.
The very latest on the contemporary art scene features at this innovative gallery, started by four local artists in the late 1990s. ◈ C/Doctor Dou 4 • Map L2 • Closed Sun & Mon

Loring Art
Multimedia and digital design are spotlighted at this trendy bookshop space. ◈ C/Gravina 8 • Map L1 • Closed Sat & Sun

The Air Shop
A range of fun inflatable products by young designers are for sale and on display here: flower vases and accessories to furniture and all kinds of personalised items. ◈ C/Angels 20 • Map K2 • Closed Sun & Mon am

Art aficionados gather at galleries for openings once a month (Tue–Thu). Enquire at individual galleries for more information.

Left **Vintage Dr Martens shoes** Right **Shop window, Revólver Records**

Vintage & Second-Hand Shops

Mies & Felj
A labour of love for two Catalan brothers and a Dutch woman, this shop is packed with vintage fur-lined leather jackets, Chinese dresses and racks of old jeans. ◊ *C/Riera Baixa 4–5 • Map K3*

HoLaLa
Rummage for an outfit at this three-floor vintage store, with everything from original silk kimonos to army pants and colourful 1950s bathing suits. ◊ *C/Tallers 73 • Map L1*

Discos Edison's
This record shop has been attracting eclectic music hounds since 1979 with a fantastic vinyl collection, including Catalan folk, Broadway tunes and Spanish pop. ◊ *C/Riera Baixa 9–10 • Map K3*

Lailo
In this theatre-turned-vintage store, you'll find everything from glitzy 1950s cocktail dresses to 1920s costumes. ◊ *C/Riera Baixa 20 • Map K3*

Revólver Records
The speciality here is classic rock – as shown by the spray-painted wall art depicting The Rolling Stones and Jimi Hendrix. One floor houses CDs, the other a huge selection of vinyl. ◊ *C/Tallers 11 • Map L2*

La Lluna de 2ª mà
Pick from a small but select array of used clothes and shoes, which may be anything from patent leather platforms to polka-dot Dr Martens. ◊ *C/Riera Baixa 10 • Map K3*

Argot
"Be original, buy original" is the motto at this jam-packed, friendly, little shop. Poke through racks of retro-wear and T-shirts printed with Mexican religious icons, Indian motifs or Mao's face. ◊ *C/Hospital 107 • Map K3*

Syndrome Barcelona
Innovative clothing by new designers includes unique recycled pieces and kitsch accessories. ◊ *Ferlandina 37 • Map K2*

Discos Tesla
This tiny, but well-stocked, record and CD store focuses on alternative music from decades past. It is the kind of place where you can hum a few lines of a song and the owner will track it down. ◊ *C/Tallers 3 • Map L2*

GI Joe Surplus
One of Spain's few army and navy surplus stores, where you can find bags, backpacks and clothing from the Russian, Israeli and US militaries. ◊ *C/Hospital 82 • Map K3*

For tips on shopping and standard opening hours **See p139**

Left **El Cafè que pone Muebles Navarro** Right **Bar Raval**

🔟 Bars & Clubs

Bar Almirall
The *Modernista* doors swing open to a young, friendly crowd at Barcelona's oldest watering hole. Founded in 1860, the bar has many original fittings, plus eclectic music and strong cocktails. ✎ *C/Joaquín Costa 33 • Map K2*

La Paloma
Elderly couples waltz across the floor early on; later, a younger set try out everything from tango to salsa. The next big things in pop often perform live *(see p67)*. ✎ *C/Tigre 27 • Map J1 • Closed Sun–Tue and for renovation until 2008*

El Cafè que pone Muebles Navarro
Kick back with a cocktail at this sprawling lounge bar speckled with low, comfortable couches. ✎ *C/Riera Alta 4–6 • Map K2 • Closed Mon*

Marsella
This dimly lit *Modernista* bar serves up cocktails and absinthe to long-time regulars and first-timers. ✎ *C/Sant Pau 65 • Map K4*

El Cangrejo
Anything from flamenco to transvestism can feature at El Cangrejo, one of the most authentic venues in El Raval. ✎ *Montserrat 9 • Map K5 • Shows 11:30pm–4:30am Fri–Sat • Closed for renovation until 2008*

Bar Raval
Presided over by a huge, papier-mâché flamenco dancer, this bar has catered to the film and theatre crowd for years. Rustic pizzas and salads are served until 2am. ✎ *C/Dr. Dou 19 • Map L2*

Moog
Big-name DJs spin techno and electronica, but for a boogie to classic '80s hits head for the second floor. ✎ *C/Arc del Teatre 3 • Map L5 • Adm*

Boadas Cocktail Bar
This smooth little cocktail bar, founded in 1933, continues to mix the meanest martinis in town for an elbow-to-elbow crowd. ✎ *C/Tallers 1 • Map L2 • Closed Sun*

London Bar
This cluttered bar has long been *de rigueur*, once with the likes of Picasso, Hemingway and Miró. Sip cocktails and enjoy live music – from jazz to folk. ✎ *C/Nou de la Rambla 34 • Map K4 • Closed Mon*

Café Teatre Llantiol
Barcelona's cabaret tradition lives on at this theatre-bar, with its flamboyant shows and *espectacles* of mime, magic and flamenco. ✎ *C/Riereta 7 • Map J3 • Shows at 9pm & 11pm Mon–Thu, 9pm, 11pm & 12:30am Fri–Sat, 6pm & 9pm Sun • Adm*

For Barcelona's best nightlife **See pp46–7**

Price Categories

For a three-course meal for one with half a bottle of wine (or equivalent meal), taxes and extra charges.

€	under €10
€€	€10–20
€€€	€20–30
€€€€	over €30

Bar Ra

🔟 Good-Value Eats

1 Casa Leopoldo
Dig into superb *mar i muntanya* fare (combining meat and fish) at this friendly, family-run restaurant. Try the meatballs with cuttlefish and shrimp. ✆ *C/Sant Rafael 24 • Map K3 • 93 441 30 14 • Closed Mon, Easter, Aug • €€€€*

2 Bar Ra
This trendy spot serves up organic goodies, from yogurt shakes to vegetarian burritos. ✆ *Pl de la Gardunya • Map L3 • 61 595 98 72 • €€€*

3 Ca L'Isidre
Picasso, Tapiès and even Woody Allen have dined on Catalan fare at this long-time artists' hang-out. ✆ *C/Flors 12 • Map J4 • 93 441 11 39 • Closed Sat (in summer), Sun, Easter, Aug, Christmas • €€€€*

4 Silenus
Tuck into Mediterranean food in a lofty space hung with local artists' work. Try the ostrich. ✆ *C/Àngels 8 • Map K2 • 93 302 26 80 • Closed Sun • €€€€*

5 Las Fernández
An informal eatery with a friendly atmosphere. The original menu features dishes from the El Bierzo area in León, such as salad with quail "lollipops". ✆ *C/Carretas 11 • Map J3 • 93 443 20 43 • Closed Mon • €€€*

6 Egipte
Boisterous diners pack this *Modernista* restaurant. Take your pick from a bewildering 60 Catalan and Mediterranean dishes. ✆ *La Rambla 79 • Map L3 • 93 317 95 45 • €€*

7 Imprevist
In an old warehouse, this café-restaurant, owned (and decorated) by Catalan artists, offers a global menu. ✆ *C/Ferlandina 34 • Map J2 • 93 342 58 59 • Closed Sat and Sun lunch • €€€*

8 Mama Cafè
Organic Mediterranean dishes (many vegetarian) are served in this airy café-restaurant, which is popular with artists. Contemporary art is projected onto the wall. ✆ *C/Doctor Dou 10 • Map L2 • 93 301 29 40 • Closed Sun eve • €€€*

9 Fonda de España
Dine on fine Catalan cuisine under a *Modernista* mosaic and dark-wood ceiling by Domènech i Montaner. Try the filet of sole flavoured with orange. ✆ *Hotel España, C/Sant Pau 9–11 • Map L4 • 93 318 17 58 • €€€€*

10 Fidel Bar
There's no better spot in El Raval for an *entrepà* (sandwich) than this old, low-ceilinged bar – opt for one with sausage and Manchego cheese. ✆ *C/Ferlandina 24 • Map K2 • No credit cards • €€*

For tips on dining and standard opening hours **See p138**

Left **Palau Nacional** Right **Estadi Olimpic**

Montjuïc

NAMED THE "JEWISH MOUNTAIN", *after an important Jewish cemetery that existed here in the Middle Ages, this sizeable and mountainous park rises 213 m (700 ft) above the port. The park itself was first landscaped for the 1929 International Exhibition, when the elegant Palau Nacional and the strikingly modern Mies van der Rohe Pavilion were also built. During the following decade, the area fell into general disuse and soon became synonymous with decline. Together with the grim shadow cast over the hill by the castle, which for years acted as a slaughterhouse for Franco's firing squads, it is little short of miraculous that Montjuïc is now one of Barcelona's biggest tourist draws. However, as the main site for the 1992 Olympics, held on its southern slopes, Montjuïc was given a comprehensive face-lift and the area was transformed into a beautiful green oasis, with two fabulous art museums and a host of stunning sports facilities.*

Statue, Castell de Montjuïc

All these elements are interconnected by a network of exterior escalators and interlaced with quiet, shady gardens, which offer dazzling views over Barcelona and a welcome respite from the bustle of the city.

🏛 Sights

1. Palau Nacional & Museu Nacional d'Art de Catalunya
2. Fundació Joan Miró
3. Font Màgica
4. Castell de Montjuïc & Museu del Cómic y la Ilustración
5. Estadi Olimpic
6. Teatre Grec
7. Palau Sant Jordi
8. Pavelló Mies van der Rohe
9. Poble Espanyol
10. Caixa Forum

For more on Barcelona's history **See pp30–31**

Fountains, Palau Nacional

1 Palau Nacional & Museu Nacional d'Art de Catalunya

The Palau Nacional is home to the Museu Nacional d'Art de Catalunya which exhibits Catalonia's historic art collections. Boasting one of Europe's finest displays of Romanesque art, the museum includes a series of breathtaking, 12th-century frescoes, rescued from Catalan Pyrenean churches and painstakingly reassembled in a series of galleries here. See pp18–19.

2 Fundació Joan Miró

One of Catalonia's most representative painters, Joan Miró (1893–1983), donated many of the 11,000 works held by the museum. Housed in a stark, white building designed by his friend, architect Josep Lluís Sert, the collection – the world's most complete array of Miro's work – was recently extended to include 25 new pieces by him. See pp22–3.

3 Font Màgica

Below the cascades and fountains that splash down from the regal Palau Nacional is the Magic Fountain, designed by Carles

Buigas for the International Exhibition of 1929. As darkness descends, countless jets of water are choreographed in a mesmerizing sound and light show. When the water meets in a single jet it can soar to 15m (50ft). The extravagant finale is often accompanied by a recording of Freddie Mercury and Montserrat Caballé singing the anthem Barcelona as the fountain fades from pink to green and back to white before silently and gracefully disappearing. ◈ Av de la Reina Maria Cristina • Map B4 • May–Sep: every 30 minutes 9:30–11:30pm Thu–Sun; Oct–Apr: every 30 minutes 7–8:30pm Fri & Sat • Free • DA

Castell de Montjuïc

4 Castell de Montjuïc & Museo del Cómic y la Ilustración

The first stone of this Baroque-style castle dominating Montjuïc's hill was laid in 1640. It was for many years a symbol of terror as a prison and torture centre for political prisoners. Today the castle houses the Museo del Cómic y la Ilustración, detailing the development of Spanish comics. There are arresting vistas, especially of the port below, as well as enchanting gardens. ◈ C/Castell • Map B6 • Open 7am–8pm daily • Museum open 10am–7pm (5pm in winter) Tue–Sun • Adm to museum

Estadi Olímpic

The Olympic Stadium was first built for the 1936 Workers' Olympics, which were cancelled with the outbreak of the Spanish Civil War *(see p31)*. Today, the original Neo-Classical façade is still in place, though the stadium was entirely rebuilt for the 1992 Olympic Games *(see p31)*. It is home to Espanyol football team *(see p61)*. The Galeria Olímpica holds mementos illustrating the importance of the games for Barcelona. ❧ *Av de l'Estadi • Map B5 • Open Jun–Sep: 10am–8pm daily; Oct–May 10am–6pm daily • Free • DA*

Teatre Grec

This beautiful, open-air amphitheatre *(see p60)* was inspired by the Classical ideas of what was known as *Noucentisme*. This late 19th-century architectural movement was a reaction to the overly-decorative nature of *Modernisme*. With its leafy, green backdrop and beautiful gardens, there are few places more enchanting than this to watch *Swan Lake* or listen to some jazz. The theatre is used for shows during the summertime Festival del Grec *(see p66)*, when it also becomes home to a luxurious outdoor restaurant. ❧ *Pg Santa Madrona • Map C4 • 10am–dusk • Free (when there are no shows)*

Palau Sant Jordi

The star of all the Olympic installations is this steel-and-glass indoor stadium *(see p66)* designed by Japanese architect Arata Isozaki. Holding around 17,000 people, the stadium is the home of the city's basketball team *(see p61)*. The esplanade – a surreal forest of concrete and metal pillars – was designed by Aiko Isozaki, Arata's wife. Further down the hill are the indoor and outdoor Bernat Picornell Olympic pools *(see p60)*; both open to the public. ❧ *Av de l'Estadi • Map A4 • Open 10am–6pm (to 8pm Jul & Aug) Sat & Sun • Free • DA*

Palau Sant Jordi

Pavelló Mies van der Rohe

You might wonder exactly what this box-like pavilion of stone, marble, onyx and glass is doing bang in the middle of Montjuïc's monumental architecture. Years ahead of its time, this surprisingly rationalist gem represents Germany's contribution to the 1929 Exhibition. Built by Ludwig Mies van der Rohe (1886–1969), the elegant pavilion was soon demolished, only to be reconstructed in 1986. Inside, the elegant sculpture *Morning* by Georg Kolbe

Barcelona Chairs, Pavelló Mies van der Rohe

You can hop on and off the Tren Turístic (see p133), which ferries visitors up the hill from Plaça d'Espanya and back. (April to October).

Poble Espanyol

(1877–1947) is reflected in a small lake. ◈ *Av Marquès de Comillas • Map B4 • Open 10am–8pm daily • Adm*

Poble Espanyol
This Spanish *poble* (village) has been recreated from a hotch-potch of scaled-down famous buildings and streets from around Spain. Although a bit tacky, it has become a centre for arts and crafts, including an impressive glass-blowers' workshop. There are restaurants and cafés aplenty, and a couple of trendy nightclubs (*see p95*). ◈ *Av Marquès de Comillas • Map A3 • Open 9am–8pm Mon, 9am–2pm Tue–Thu, 9am–4am Fri, 9am–5pm Sat, 9am–midnight Sun • Adm*

Caixa Forum
The Fundació La Caixa's impressive collection of contemporary art is housed in a former textile factory, designed by *Modernista* architect Puig i Cadafalch. The collection began in 1985 and assembles some 800 works by Spanish and foreign artists, which are shown in rotation along with temporary international exhibitions. ◈ *Av Marquès de Comillas • Map B3 • Open 10am–8pm Tue–Sun • Free • DA*

A Day in Montjuïc

Morning

To get to the **Fundació Joan Miró** *(see pp22–3)* before the crowds and with energy to spare, hop on the funicular from Paral·lel metro station. From here it is a short walk to the museum, where you'll need an hour and a half to absorb the impressive collection of Miró paintings, sketches and sculptures. When you've had your fill of contemporary art, refuel with a *cafè amb llet (see p43)* on the restaurant terrace before backtracking along Av de Miramar and jumping on the cable car up to **Castell de Montjuïc** *(see p89)*. Wander the castle gardens and look out over the city and the bustling docks. Return to Av de Miramar by cable car and follow the signs to the **Palau Nacional** *(see p89)*, where you can lunch on typical Catalan cuisine with a modern twist in the grandiose Oval Room *(see p93)*.

Afternoon

Afterwards, spend an hour perusing the **MNAC**'s *(see pp18–19)* extraordinary Romanesque art collection. When you exit, turn right and then follow the signs to the Olympic complex. The **Estadi Olímpic** is worth a look, but the silver-domed **Palau Sant Jordi** steals the limelight. Nearby, at Bernat Picornell, spend the late afternoon cooling down with a dip in the fantastic open-air pool. If it's summer, there may even be a film showing. From here it is just a short stroll to the **Poble Espanyol** where you can settle in at a terrace bar in Plaça de Mayor and sip a *cuba libre* as night descends.

Around Town – Montjuïc

 Following pages **13th-century altar frontal, Museu Nacional d'Art de Catalunya**

PAR. BALTASAR. MELCHIOR

Left **Jardins Mossèn Jacint Verdaguer** Right **Castell Jardins**

🔟 Parks & Gardens

1 Jardins Mossèn Costa i Llobera

These are among Europe's most important cactus gardens. They are particularly impressive as the sun sets, when surreal and shapes and shadows emerge. ◈ Map C5

2 Jardí Botànic

These wild gardens offer splendid vistas and hundreds of examples of typical Mediterranean vegetation. ◈ Map A4 • Open Apr, May, Sep: 10am–6pm daily (to 8pm Sat & Sun); Jun–Aug: 10am–8pm daily; Oct–Mar: 10am–5pm daily • Adm; free last Sun of month

3 Jardins Mossèn Cinto Verdaguer

The best time to visit these wonderfully elegant gardens is in spring when the plants are in blossom and the colours and aromas are in full force. ◈ Map C5

4 Jardins del Castell

Cannons among the rose bushes, and pathways along the walls of a flower-filled moat, are the highlights of these gardens, which ring the castle. ◈ Map B5

5 Jardins del Teatre Grec

Reminiscent of the Hanging Gardens of Babylon, this gracious oasis surrounding the Greek amphitheatre is officially known as La Rosadela. ◈ Map C4

6 Jardins de Miramar

Opposite the Miramar, with its telescopes and viewing spots, these gardens are scattered with stairways leading to enchanting leafy groves with vistas. ◈ Map C5

7 Jardins Laribal

This multi-level park hides a small *Modernista* house, by Puig i Cadafalch, and the Font del Gat – a drinking fountain, which has inspired many local songs. ◈ Map B4

8 Jardins de Joan Maragall

An avenue lined with sculptures by Frederic Marès and Ernest Maragall is the main delight here. The garden also has the last of the city's *ginjoler* trees. ◈ Map B4 • Open 10am–6pm Sat & Sun

9 Muntanya de Montjuïc

A multitude of secret paths leads through wild gardens on Montjuïc's south side, the only part of the mountain that remains untamed. ◈ Map A5

10 El Mirador del Llobregat

A viewing area with small gardens nearby, this is the only place in the city where you can see the plains of the Llobregat stretching below. ◈ Map A3 • DA

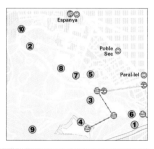

Unless otherwise stated, parks & gardens are usually open 10am–dusk daily.

Price Categories

For a three-course meal for one with half a bottle of wine (or equivalent meal), taxes and extra charges.

€ under €10
€€ €10–€20
€€€ €20–€30
€€€€ over €30

Interior, Font de Prades

🔟 Restaurants, Cafés, Bars & Clubs

1 MNAC Café
The grand Oval Room of the Palau Nacional is an elegant lunching spot. Specialities include vegetables au gratin and pastries. ◈ *Parc de Montjuïc • Map 4 • Closed eve • DA • €€*

2 Cañota
Cañota's superb, traditional, and supremely economical cooking includes excellent game dishes. This place lives up to its phenomenal reputation. ◈ *C/Lleida 7 • Map C4 • 93 325 91 71 • DA • €€€€*

3 Fundació Joan Miró Restaurant
A great terrace, views of Miró's sculptures, plus well-presented modern food with an Italian accent. ◈ *Parc de Montjuïc • Map B5 • 93 329 07 68 • Closed eve • DA • €€*

4 Rias de Galicia
A giant aquarium is full of lobster, crabs and more, all waiting to be plucked out and served up fresh and sizzling on a plate. ◈ *C/ Lleida 9 • Map C4 • 93 424 81 52 • €€€€*

5 Cala Santa Maria
A bit off the beaten track, but worth hunting out, this authentic Spanish eatery offers an excellent selection of tapas. ◈ *C/Guadiana 12 • Map B2 • 93 421 87 05 • Closed lunch & Mon • €€*

6 L'Albi
Looking out over the Poble's "village square", this huge terrace restaurant offers stunning views and a good range of traditional Mediterranean dishes. ◈ *Poble Espanyol • Map A3 • 93 424 93 24 • €€€*

7 La Terrrazza
Techno music rules at one of Barcelona's most popular nightclubs, housed in a Balearic-style mansion inside the Poble Espanyol. ◈ *Poble Espanyol • Map A3 • Closed Sun–Wed in winter • Adm*

8 Font de Prades
By far the best food in the Poble Espanyol. ◈ *Poble Espanyol • Map A3 • 93 426 75 19 • Closed Mon • €€€*

9 Bar Miramar
No prizes for the chicken-and-chips style cuisine, but Miramar scores with its unbeatable city views. ◈ *Av de Miramar • Map C5 • €*

10 Restaurant Martí
A typical local restaurant with a fantastically economical three-course lunch in pleasant and unpretentious surroundings. ◈ *Consell de Cent 38–40 • Map B3 • 93 325 75 15 • DA • Closed Sun eve • €€€€*

Left **L'Aquàrium** Right **Swing Bridge, between La Rambla & Moll D'Espanya**

Port Vell, Barceloneta & Port Olímpic

THE HEADY ALLURE OF THE MEDITERRANEAN *permeates Barcelona, and a dip into its azure waters is only a few metro stops (or a brisk walk) away. Barcelona's beaches were once hidden behind an industrial wasteland, but things changed radically in preparation for the 1992 Olympics. The rallying cry was to create a new Barcelona oberta al mar (open to the sea); the result is phenomenal, as is the presence of large crowds seeking sun and sea. Tons of sand were transported to create miles of silky beaches from the fisherman's quarter of Barceloneta to Port Olímpic and beyond. Palm trees were planted, water cleanliness standards implemented and, this being design-obsessed Barcelona, numerous contemporary sculptures erected. The city's first two skyscrapers, the Torre Mapfre office building and the five-star Hotel Arts (see p143), punctuate the port's skyline, while the nearby Port Olímpic throbs with the highest concentration of bars and clubs in the city.*

Barceloneta beach

🔟 Sights & Attractions

1. Beaches
2. Museu d'Història de Catalunya
3. Rambla de Mar
4. L'Aquàrium
5. Barceloneta
6. Boat & Cable Car Trips
7. Pailebot Santa Eulàlia
8. Submarine Ictineo II
9. El Centre de la Vila-Port Olímpic
10. World Trade Center

Take a boat tour of the port area See p133

Beaches

Fancy a splash in the Mediterranean? Trot down to the end of La Rambla, wander along the palm tree-lined Moll de la Fusta, down restaurant-packed Passeig Joan de Borbó, *et voilà*, the sea beckons. Over four km (2.5 miles) of blue flag beaches stretch north from Barceloneta to Port Olímpic and beyond. Facilities are top-notch, including showers, deck chairs, beach volleyball courts and lifeguards. Convenience, however, means crowds, so finding a spot among the masses of oiled bodies can be a challenge, particularly in the summer. ◈ *Map E6*

Museu d'Història de Catalunya

Housed in the Palau de Mar, a renovated portside warehouse, this museum offers a broad, interactive exploration of Catalonia's history since prehistoric times. Kids *(see p63)* especially will have a ball with the engaging exhibits, such as a Civil War-era bunker and a recreated Catalan bar from the 1960s with an ancient *futbolín* (table football) game. ◈ *Pl Pau Vila 3, Palau de Mar • Map N6 • Open 10am–7pm Tue–Sat (until 8pm Wed), 10am–2:30pm Sun • Adm €3, free first Sun of month • DA*

Rambla de Mar

Saunter along the Rambla de Mar, a floating wooden pier that leads to Maremagnum, a flashy mall of shops, fast-food outlets, restaurants and bars. Nearby the giant IMAX® cinema shows 3-D films on mega-screens, generally on nature-,

Museu d'Història de Catalunya

adventure-, and sports-related topics. ◈ *Moll d'Espanya • Map E5* ◈ *Maremagnum: Open 10am–10pm daily* ◈ *IMAX: shows from noon–11:30pm daily • Adm • DA*

L'Aquàrium

Come face to face with the teeming marine world of the Mediterranean at Barcelona's impressive aquarium, the largest in Europe. The highlight is an 80-m (262-ft) long underwater tunnel equipped with a moving walkway that transports visitors through the deep blue unknown, while sharks glide menacingly close. A huge hit with the kids is the new Explora! floor, with interactive activities that allow you to explore the ecosystems of the Mediterranean.
◈ *Moll d'Espanya • Map E6 • Open Jul–Aug: 9:30am–11pm daily; Sep–Jun: 9:30am–9:30pm daily • Adm*

Yachts, Port Olímpic

The rooftop café at the Museu d'Història de Catalunya has sweeping views of the city, the port area & Montjuïc.

Barceloneta

A portside warren of narrow streets, small squares and ancient bars, this traditional neighbourhood of *pescadors* (fishermen) and *mariners* (sailors) seems worlds apart from the megamalls and disco lights of nearby Port Olímpic. A refreshing foray through this tight-knit community yields a glimpse into

Yachts & skyscrapers, Port Olímpic

the way Barcelona was 150 years ago. Older couples still pull chiars out onto the street to gossip and watch the world go by, and small seafood restaurants serve a *menú del dia* of whatever's fresh off the boat. Running the length of Barceloneta's western edge is Passeig Joan de Borbó, which is lined with restaurants serving *mariscs* (shellfish) and paellas. ⬙ *Map F5*

Boat & Cable Car Trips

See Barcelona's port activity from a different perspective, either from the air or the sea. The *telefèric* cable cars offer

Street scene, Barceloneta

sweeping bird's-eye views of Barcelona and its coast, while the old-fashioned Les Golondrines boats and the Orsom Catamaran sweep you around the port area. ⬙ *Telefèric, from Torre Jaume I & Torre San Sebastià • Map D6 & E6 • Adm* ⬙ *Les Golondrines, Portal de la Pau • Map E5 • roughly 30 mins from 11:30am • 93 442 31 06 • Adm* ⬙ *Orsom Catamaran, Portal de la Pau • Map E5 • Call 93 441 05 37 for times • Adm • DA*

Pailebot Santa Eulàlia

Bobbing in the water at the Moll de la Fusta (Timber Quay) is this renovated, three-mast schooner, originally christened *Carmen Flores*. It first set sail from Spain in 1918. On journeys to Cuba, the ship used to transport textiles and salt, and return with tobacco, coffee, cereals and wood. In 1997, the Museu Marítim *(see p81)* bought and restored the ship as part of an ongoing project to create a collection of seaworthy historical Catalan vessels. ⬙ *Moll de la Fusta • Map L6 • Open noon–7pm Tue–Sun (from 10am Sat & Sun; to 5:30pm in winter) • Adm*

Submarine Ictíneo II

In 1859, Catalan Narcís Monturiol invented one of the world's first submarines, a replica of which stands on the Moll d'Espanya. Hard to believe, but in an earlier version of this wooden, fish-shaped submarine, powered by two internal steam engines, Monturiol made a number of successful underwater journeys.

He invented the submarine as a means of gathering coral; later, he tried to sell it to the army. However, he finally sold his invention in parts and died penniless. ⊗ *Moll d'Espanya • Map E5*

9 El Centre de la Vila-Port Olímpic

This large shopping complex offers a slew of shops, cafés and fast food restaurants. Best of all, it houses the cinemas of the Icària Yelmo Cineplex *(see p67)*, one of the largest cinemas in town to show VO (non-dubbed) films. ⊗ *Salvador Espriu 61 • Map H5*
• Mall shops open 10am–10pm Mon–Sat

Pailebot Santa Eulàlia

10 World Trade Center

This massive, circular structure is home to offices, convention halls, a five-star hotel and the top-notch restaurant Ruccula *(see p101)*. There are also several gift shops, including Galería Surrealista, featuring souvenirs inspired by Dalí and other Surrealists. In the central courtyard is a "rhythmic" fountain that spurts out streams of water at differing velocities. Nearby, you can board cable cars and soak up splendid views from the top of Torre Jaume I. ⊗ *Moll de Barcelona • Map D6 • DA*

Exploring the Port

Morning

Begin your port *passeig* (stroll) with a visit to the **Museu Marítim** *(see p81)*, where you can see Barcelona's status as one of the most active ports in the Mediterranean. From here, head towards the Monument a Colom *(see p12)*, and stroll the Moll de la Fusta to admire the **Pailebot Santa Eulàlia**, which has been immaculately restored by the museum. Saunter down the **Rambla de Mar** *(see p97)*, an undulating wooden drawbridge that leads to the glitzy Maremagnum mega-mall. At the start of the pier, embark on the **Orsom Catamaran**, where you can grab a drink and snack and soak up the rays and the port skyline, while sprawled out on a net just inches above the water. Back on land, about 90 minutes later, stroll down the Moll d'Espanya and turn towards the traditional fisherman's quarter of **Barceloneta**, an atmospheric pocket of narrow streets and timeworn bars. Get a real taste of old-style Barcelona at the boisterous tapas bar, **El Vaso de Oro** (C/Balboa 6). Wedge yourself in at the bar and savour some tasty seafood morsels.

Afternoon

Revived, head to Pg Joan de Borbó and make for the beach. Douse yourself in the Med, then siesta in the afternoon sun. Pick yourself up with sangria at the beachside **Salamanca Chiringuito** (at the end of Pg Joan de Borbó), where you can bury your feet in the sand and watch the waves lap on the shore as the sun dips into the horizon.

You can't miss Frank Gehry's massive, glistening Peix sculpture on Passeig Marítim **See p41**

Left **Pachito** Right **Razzmatazz**

🔟 Bars & Beach Clubs

Club Catwalk
One of the hottest clubs in town, this has two floors: one for the bar and chilling out, and the other for dancing to music that is strictly electronic and house. ⊗ *Ramón Trías Fargas 2–4 • Map G6 • Closed Mon–Wed • DA • Adm*

CDLC
Right by the beach, with a terrace on which to relax, this is a restaurant that becomes a club after dinner. Guest DJs feature every week. ⊗ *Passeig Marítim de la Barceloneta 32 • Map G6*

Pachito
One of the first clubs on the Port Olímpic strip, this buzzing nightspot pumps techno and Latin house to a lively crowd. ⊗ *Moll Mistral 43 • Map G5*

Kennedy Irish Sailing Club
When you tire of dance music, try this open-air Irish bar with live rock and pop bands every night and sport on big TVs. ⊗ *Moll Mistral 26–27 • Map G5 • Closed Mon*

Baja Beach
Good-looking beach boys and girls encourage everyone to dance in this Californian-style beach club. Meals are served on the terrace overlooking the sea. ⊗ *Passeig Marítim de la Barceloneta 34 • Map G6 • Closed Mon–Wed*

Le Kasbah
With Arabic decoration, soft lights and house music, this bar in the Palau del Mar building provides a city oasis. ⊗ *Plaça de Pau Vila 1 • Map F6 • Closed Mon*

Salsa
Salsa turns up the heat at this often-heaving spot, where Latino music lovers flock to flirt and dance. ⊗ *Moll Mistral 21 • Map G5*

Cafè & Cafè
Before hitting the clubs, get fired up on caffeine or cocktails at this café-bar, full of antiques from the former Yugoslavia, birthplace of the original owner. ⊗ *Moll Mistral 30 • Map G5*

Shôko
A Japanese restaurant during the day, this club by the beach provides all kinds of music in a great setting. ⊗ *Passeig Marítim de la Barceloneta 36 • Map E6 • Closed Mon–Wed*

Razzmatazz
Concerts – from rock to jazz – feature several nights a week at this trendy club. On Fridays and Saturdays, Razz Club is alternative. The Loft next door (run by the same people) plays electronica and techno. ⊗ *C/Almogàvers 122 (The Loft: C/Pamplona 88) • Map H4 • Closed Sun–Thu*

 For Barcelona's best nightlife **See pp46–7**

Price Categories

For a three-course meal for one with half a bottle of wine (or equivalent meal), taxes and extra charges.

€ up to €10
€€ €10–20
€€€ €20–30
€€€€ over €30

Paella, Can Ramonet

🔟 Restaurants & Tapas Bars

1 Set Portes
Founded in 1836, this large institution serves some of the finest Catalan cuisine in the city, including robust paellas. ✪ *Pg Isabel II 14 • Map N5 • 93 319 30 33 • DA • €€€€*

2 Agua
The spacious terrace at this restaurant boasts views of the sea. Superb seafood and Mediterranean fare feature on the menu. ✪ *Pg Marítim 30 • Map G6 • 93 225 12 72 • DA • €€€€*

3 Can Manel la Puda
The oldest restaurant on this strip serves time-honoured Catalan cuisine, specializing in catch-of-the-day dishes. ✪ *Pg Joan de Borbó 60–61 • Map F6 • 93 221 50 13 • €€€*

4 Somorrostro
This chic restaurant serves a daily changing menu prepared with fresh ingredients. Young ambience and warm decor. ✪ *Sant Carles 11 • Map F6 • 93 225 00 10 • Closed lunch (except Sun), Tue • €€€*

5 Can Ramonet
One of the oldest restaurants in the area, this place serves seafood and paella, including their signature paella *Can Ramonet*, piled with seafood and meat. ✪ *C/Maquinista 17 • Map F6 • 93 319 30 64 • Closed last two weeks Jan • €€€€*

6 Reial Club Marítim Restaurant
The yacht club's restaurant offers views of the harbour and a top-notch seafood menu. ✪ *Moll d'Espanya • Map E6 • 93 221 62 56 • Closed Sun eve & Mon • €€€€*

7 Can Ganassa
An old-style, family-run tapas bar that has been serving fresh seafood tapas to locals for decades. ✪ *Pl de la Barceloneta 4–6 • Map F6 • 93 225 19 97 • €€*

8 Andaira
On the seafront of Barceloneta. The cuisine has a creative, international flair. Sweet roasted scallops with truffle-perfumed mash is recommended. ✪ *Vilajoiosa 52–54 • Map F6 • 93 221 16 16 • €€€€*

9 Suquet de l'Almirall
This family-run gem serves excellent *arroz de barca* (rice in broth, with seafood) and *suquet* (seafood and potato stew). ✪ *Pg Joan de Borbó 63 • Map F6 • 93 221 62 33 • Closed Sun eve, Mon, three weeks Aug • DA • €€€€*

10 Sugar Club
Innovative Mediterranean and French food – try rillettes of duck confit with gherkins – makes this a hit. ✪ *World Trade Center, Moll de Barcelona • Map D6 • 93 508 82 68 • Closed Mon eve, Tue eve, Sat lunch, Sun • DA • €€€€*

Unless otherwise stated, all restaurants accept credit cards.
For tips on dining and standard opening hours See p138

Left **Fountain, Rambla de Catalunya** Right *Modernista* hotel entrance

Eixample

IF THE OLD TOWN IS THE HEART of Barcelona and the green mountains of Tibidabo and Montjuïc the lungs, the Eixample is the city's nervous system – its economic and commercial core. The area began to take shape in 1860 when the city was permitted to expand beyond the medieval walls (see p30). Its design, based on plans by Catalan engineer Ildefons Cerdà, comprises hundreds of symmetrical grid-like squares. Construction continued into the 20th century at a time when Barcelona's elite was patronizing the city's most daring architects. Modernisme was flourishing and the area became home to the cream of Barcelona's Modernista architecture, with myriad elegant façades and balconies. Today, a wealth of enchanting cafés, funky design shops, gourmet restaurants and hip bars and clubs draws the professional crowd, which has adopted the neighbourhood as its own.

10 Sights

1. Sagrada Família
2. La Pedrera
3. Mansana de la Discòrdia
4. Hospital de la Santa Creu i de Sant Pau
5. Fundació Tàpies
6. Palau Macaya
7. Fundació Francisco Godia
8. Rambla de Catalunya
9. Universitat de Barcelona
10. Museu Egipci

Spires, Sagrada Família

For more on Modernista architecture **See pp32–3**

1 Sagrada Família

Gaudí's wizardry culminated in this enchanting, wild, unconventional temple, which dominates the city skyline (see pp8–10).

2 La Pedrera

A daring, surreal fantasyland, and Gaudí's most remarkable civic work (see pp20–21).

3 Mansana de la Discòrdia

At the heart of the city's *Quadrat d'Or* (Golden Square) lies this stunning block of houses. Literally "the block of discord", the Mansana de la Discòrdia is so-called because of the dramatic contrast of its three flagship buildings. Built between 1900 and 1907 by the three *Modernista* greats, rival architects Gaudí, Domènech i Montaner and Puig i Cadafalch, the buildings were commissioned by competing bourgeois families. Domènech is represented by the ornate Casa Lleó Morera (see p33); Puig makes his mark with the Gothic-inspired Casa Amatller (see p33); and Gaudí flaunts his architectural prowess with Casa Batlló (see p33). All boast superb interiors – sadly closed to the public – with the exception of Casa Batlló. The lesser-known houses at Nos. 37 and 39 add to the overall splendour of the block.

Windows, Casa Batlló, Mansana de la Discòrdia

The Perfume Museum at No. 39 is heaven for scent-lovers (see p41). ◈ Pg de Gràcia 35–45 • Map E2

4 Hospital de la Santa Creu i de Sant Pau

It's almost worth feigning illness to be admitted to this fully functioning hospital, which was built in two stages from 1905 by Domènech i Montaner and his son. A tribute to *Modernisme* – and Domènech's answer to Gaudí's Sagrada Família – the sumptuous design comprises eight pavilions and various other buildings linked by underground tunnels. The pavilions, each different, recall the history of Catalonia with murals, mosaics and sculptures. Interlacing the buildings are gardens creating beautiful outdoor oases, where patients can recuperate. The courtyards and gardens are open to visitors. ◈ C/Sant Antoni Maria Claret 167 • Map H1

Left **Hospital de la Santa Creu i de Sant Pau** Right **Casa Lleó Morera, Mansana de la Discòrdia**

 For more on Antoni Gaudí See p11

Courtyard, Palau Macaya

Fundació Tàpies

Paintings and sculptures by Antoni Tàpies (b. 1923), Catalonia's foremost living artist, are housed in this early *Modernista* building *(see p32)*. For a glimpse of what awaits inside, look up: crowning the museum is the artist's eye-catching wire sculpture *Cloud & Chair* (1990). The collection of over 300 pieces covers Tàpies' whole range of work, including impressive abstract pieces such as *Grey Ochre on Brown* (1962). Temporary exhibitions are also held here, with past shows by Mario Herz, Hans Hacke and Craigie Horsfield. ✆ *C/Aragó 255* • *Map E2* • *Open 10am–8pm Tue–Sun* • *Adm €6 (con €4)* • *DA* • *Free under 16*

Palau Macaya

Designed by Puig i Cadafalch (1901), this palace is a fine example of the Neo-Gothic style in *Modernista* architecture. A magical, white façade is broken up by engravings and two towers. Of note are the decorative sculptures by *Modernista* sculptor Eusebi Arnau. The palace belongs to the Centre Cultural de la Caixa and, unfortunately, is closed at the moment; it is, however, worth a visit to see the outside alone. ✆ *Pg Sant Joan 108* • *Map F2*

Ildefons Cerdà

Ildefons Cerdà's design for the new city, comprising a uniform grid of square blocks, received backing in 1859. Reflecting Cerdà's utopian socialist ideals, each block was to have a garden-like courtyard, surrounded by uniform flats. Real estate vultures soon intervened and the court-yards were converted into warehouses and factories. Today these green spaces are gradually being reinstated.

Fundació Francisco Godia

Although Francisco Godia (1921–90) was best known for his prowess behind the wheel – notably as an F1 racing driver – his passions extended to the art world. His once private collection now forms this museum and encompasses a range of art from medieval times to the 20th-century: from Jaume Huguet's altarpiece *St Mary Magdalene* (c. 1445) to a range of Spanish ceramics and works by 17th-century fresco-painter Luca Giordano. ✆ *C/Valencia 284* • *Map E2* • *Open 10am–2pm, 4–7pm Mon & Wed–Sat, 10am–2pm Sun* • *Adm*

Cloud & Chair sculpture, Fundació Tàpies

Rambla de Catalunya

This elegant extension of the better-known Rambla is a more up-market version. Lined with trees that form a leafy green tunnel in summer, it boasts scores of pretty façades and shops, including the *Modernista* Farmàcia Bolos (No. 77). The avenue teems with terrace bars and cafés, which are ideal for people-watching. *See also p50.* ⊗ *Map E2*

Interior courtyard, Universitat de Barcelona

Universitat de Barcelona

Until 1958, this was the only university in Barcelona – today it is one of six. The graceful building (1861–1889) occupies two blocks of the Eixample and has a distinct air of academia. The interior gardens with their fountains and patios make for a cool, shady hideaway on hot afternoons. ⊗ *Pl de la Universitat • Map E3*

Museu Egipci

Spain's most important Egyptology museum houses more than 350 exhibits from over 3,000 years of Ancient Egypt. Exhibits include terracotta figures, human and animal mummies, and a bust of the lion goddess Sekhmet (700–300 BC). ⊗ *C/Valencia 284 • Map E2 • Open 10am–8pm Mon–Sat, 10am–2pm Sun • Adm €7 (con €5)*

The Modernista Route

Morning

🕐 Pop into the decrepit chess bar El Pato Loco (cnr Diputació & Aribau) to get a sepia picture of Barcelona that hasn't changed for a century. Wake up with a *café solo* and watch the old men playing speed-chess, then stroll around the gardens of the **Universitat** Head east along Gran Via past the elegant Palace Barcelona Hotel *(see p143)* and right down C/Bruc for your first real taste of Catalan Art Nouveau, with Gaudí's **Casa Calvet** *(see p107)* on C/Casp. Turn right onto C/Casp and walk three blocks west to the majestic Pg de Gràcia; then go right again three blocks to the impressive buildings known as the **Mansana de la Discòrdia** *(see p103)* and the **Perfume Museum** *(see p41).* Sniff around **Regia** perfume shop *(see p106)* before continuing north to marvel at Gaudí's **La Pedrera** *(see pp20–21).* Feeling peckish? Stop at **Tragaluz** on Ptge de la Concepció *(see p107).* The set menu is an economical way to experience this glitterati hang-out.

Afternoon

After lunch, head north on Pg de Gràcia, turn right along Diagonal, taking in the fairy-tale **Casa de les Punxes** at No. 416 *(see p33).* Walk along Diagonal, making a detour left at Pg Sant Joan to see **Palau Macaya** at No. 108. Then stroll along C/Mallorca to the **Sagrada Família** *(see pp8–11).* Here you can take in the Nativity Façade and rest weary legs in the Plaça de Gaudí before climbing the bell towers for a breathtaking view of the city.

Left **Light, Dos i Una** Centre **Shoppers, Passeig de Gràcia** Right **Furniture, Vinçon**

Design Shops

1 Vinçon
The cream of the crop in Spanish design with out-of-this-world designs for the most everyday objects. Furniture is displayed in a 1900 upper-class apartment. Breathtaking. ⊗ *Pg de Gràcia 96 • Map E2*

2 Favorita
Superb design shop in *Modernista* Casa Thomas, selling the best in Catalan furniture. Worth a visit to see the exhibition furniture by the likes of Gaudí and Dalí. ⊗ *C/Mallorca 291 • Map F2*

3 Regia
The biggest perfume shop in the city has more than a thousand scents, including all the leading brands and other surprises. Also home to the Perfume Museum *(see p41)*. ⊗ *Pg de Gràcia 39 • Map E2*

4 Dos i Una
A designer gift shop with a steel-tiled floor and a psychedelic colour scheme. Concentrates on selling "made in Barcelona" items, which make for unusual souvenirs. ⊗ *C/Rosselló 275 • Map E2*

5 Muxart
Excellent and arty shoe shop for men, women and kids in a country famed for its leather. ⊗ *C/Rosselló 230 • Map E2*

6 Biosca & Botey
Exceptionally elegant shop selling all kinds of lamps, from Art-Nouveau mushrooms to ultra-modern steel shades. ⊗ *Rambla de Catalunya 125 • Map E2 • DA*

7 Pilma
Breathtaking designer shop selling quality modern furniture and interior accessories by big names, as well as cuttting-edge creations by Catalan designers. ⊗ *Av Diagonal 403 • Map E1*

8 D Barcelona
An eclectic range of gadgets and gifts in a shop that doubles as an exhibition space for up-and-coming designers and more established artists. ⊗ *Av Diagonal 367 • Map F2*

9 Kowasa
A specialist photography bookshop with over 7,000 titles, including foreign magazines. The ambience is friendly and intimate and browsing is encouraged. ⊗ *C/Mallorca 235 • Map E2 • DA*

10 Sadur
The owner designs and sells her own leather accessories: wallets, bags and a few gifts. Classy designs are well made and well priced. ⊗ *C/Bruc 150 • Map F2*

Nightlife in the Eixample

TOP 10 After-Dark Venues

1 La Fira
Decked out in vintage fairground memorabilia, this striking bar rates high on novelty factor. Order a *cuba libre* while swaying in a swing. Lively atmosphere, unique setting. ◈ *C/Provença 171 • Map D2 • Closed Mon • Adm*

2 Sala B
A smartly decorated place with intimate corners for romantic conversations. Come here for 1970s and '80s music and live acts on Thursdays and Fridays. ◈ *C/Muntaner 244 • Map D1 • Closed Sun–Wed • DA*

3 Dry Martini
A classic and elegant venue where extraordinarily professional barmen are ready to prepare your favourite cocktail. Quiet jazz sounds play in the background. ◈ *C/Aribau 162 • Map D2*

4 Nick Havanna
A classic designer spot with some outré toilets and a fabulous cow-skin upholstered bar. The crowd is mostly yuppie and moneyed. ◈ *C/Rosselló 208 • Map E2*

5 Velvet
Large, popular and populist disco bar with lavish decor, luxury fittings and music ranging from Elvis to Abba. ◈ *C/Balmes 161 • Map E2 • Adm*

6 Luz de Gas
A classic late-night watering hole, this half concert hall, half bar has live music nightly – from blues to jazz and soul. ◈ *C/Muntaner 246 • Map D1 • DA*

7 Ideal
Luxurious cocktail lounge opened by legendary barman José María Gotarda in the 1950s and now run by his son. More than 80 varieties of whisky. ◈ *C/Aribau 89 • Map D2*

8 La Bodegueta
This unassuming basement bodega has become a major pre-party meeting point. Famously good anchovies. ◈ *Rambla de Catalunya 100 • Map E2*

9 Dietrich Gay Teatro Café
A trendy gay club with a mixed door policy and a beautiful internal garden. It plays house and garage, and holds shows by singers, trapeze artists and acrobats. ◈ *Consell de Cent 255 • Map D3*

10 Les Gens que j'Aime
The ideal place to have a drink, to the accompaniment of soft music, after walking around Paseo de Gràcia and Rambla Catalunya. ◈ *Valencia 286 • Map E2 • 6pm–2:30am daily (3am weekends)*

For Barcelona's best nightlife **See pp46–7**

107

Left **Laie Llibreria Cafè** Right **Casa Alfonso**

TOP10 Cafés

Laie Llibreria Cafè
A cultural meeting place with a lively atmosphere, airy terrace and foreign newspapers. There's an excellent set lunch and live jazz (Mar–May: Tue). ◈ *C/Pau Claris 85 • Map E3 • Closed Sun*

Cafè del Centre
Said to be the oldest café in the Eixample, with dark wooden interiors that have not changed for a century. An unpretentious and authentic spot for a quiet coffee. ◈ *C/Girona 69 • Map F3 • Closed after 9pm*

Casa Alfonso
This classy café has been in business since 1929. Arguably the best *pernil* (serrano ham) in the city. ◈ *C/Roger de Llúria 6 • Map F3 • Closed Sun*

Cacao Sampaka
An infinite array of chocolate, including innovative combinations such as chocolate with Parmesan cheese or olive oil. ◈ *C/Consell de Cent 292 • Map E3 • Closed Sun*

Mauri
One of the best pastry shops in town. Enjoy a hot drink with an elaborate dessert in *Modernista* surroundings. ◈ *Rambla Catalunya 102 • Map E2 • Closed Sun eve*

Bar Paris
Chaotic and lively, with a sunny terrace, Bar Paris attracts a student crowd. Open 24 hours a day, seven days a week, it's ideal for clubbers not ready to go home. ◈ *C/Paris 187 • Map D1*

Palace Barcelona
This elegant *Modernista* hotel is the perfect place for breakfast in the conservatory or afternoon tea in the Grand Hall. It's thoroughly luxurious, but pricey. ◈ *Gran Via de les Cortes Catalanes 668 • Map F3 • DA*

Bauma
A mixed crowd drifts in to read the paper or smoke a Havana cigar with a post-lunch *carajillo* (coffee and cognac). ◈ *C/Roger de Llúria 124 • Map F2 • Closed Sat • DA*

Mantequería Ravell
A deli-style shop offering incredible breakfasts, including eggs with foie gras, at a huge communal table. Wine and traditional hams and cheeses are also available. ◈ *C/Aragó 313 • Map F2 • Closed Mon & Sat after 6pm, Tue & Wed after 9pm, Sun*

Tragarrapid
This newly opened spot is one of the most chic cafés in town. Up-market tapas and coffee served with style. ◈ *Ptge de la Concepció 5 • Map E2*

Price Categories

For a three-course meal for one with half a bottle of wine (or equivalent meal), taxes and extra charges.

€	up to €10
€€	€10–20
€€€	€20–30
€€€€	over €30

Table setting, Eixample restaurant

🔟 Restaurants & Tapas Bars

1 Tragaluz
The who's who of Barcelona wine and dine in this design-conscious, three-floored restaurant. Imaginative Mediterranean menu. ❧ Ptge de la Concepció 5 • Map E2 • 93 487 01 96 • €€€€

2 La Semproniana
Set in an old printworks, this place serves food that's a cross between Catalan and nouvelle cuisine – with a sense of playfulness. Try the black pudding lasagne. ❧ C/Rosselló 148 • Map E2 • 93 453 18 20 • Closed Sun • €€€€ • DA

3 Miranda
The emphasis at Barcelona's first decidedly gay restaurant is on the drag queen acts, not the economical International food. ❧ C/Casanova 30 • Map D3 • 93 453 52 49 • Closed Sat lunch, Sun • €€€€

4 L'Olivé
An unassuming, family-style restaurant with excellent, well-priced regional cuisine. Reputedly the best place to eat that Catalan speciality pig's trotter. The broad bean salad with mint is recommended. ❧ C/Balmes 47 • Map E3 • 934 52 19 90 • Closed Sun eve • €€€€

5 El Japonés
El Japonés pulls in a lively, hip crowd to feast on sushi, sashimi and tempura at communal trestle tables. Low lighting, buzzy atmosphere. ❧ Ptge de la Concepció 2 • Map E2 • 93 487 25 92 • €€€ • DA

6 Casa Calvet
Splurge on Catalan food with a modern twist and fine wine in the impressive surroundings of these Gaudí-designed dining rooms. ❧ C/Casp 48 • Map F3 • 93 412 40 12 • Closed Sun • €€€€ • DA

7 La Flauta
An economical, any-time-of-day option serving hundreds of types of flauta (thin baguettes). ❧ C/Aribau 23 • Map D3 • 93 323 70 38 • Closed Sun • €

8 Qu Qu
Hugely popular tapas; the three-cheese croquettes hit the spot. ❧ Pg de Gràcia 24 • Map E3 • 93 317 45 12 • €€ • DA

9 Cervecería Catalana
Just a few steps from Rambla de Catalunya, with some of the best tapas in town and a variety of domestic and imported beers. ❧ C/Mallorca 236 • Map E2 • 93 216 03 68 • €€€ • DA

10 El Principal
Oriental in design with a great terrace and "new" Mediterranean food. ❧ C/Provença 286 • Map E2 • 93 272 0845 • €€€€ • DA

Unless otherwise stated, all restaurants accept credit cards.
For tips on dining and standard opening hours See p138

109

Left **Cloister, Monestir de Pedralbes** Right **Exterior, Monestir de Pedralbes**

Gràcia, Tibidabo & Zona Alta

THE ZONA ALTA (Uptown) is an area covering several neighbourhoods that, as the name suggests, are in the hilly part of the city. From the moneyed streets of Pedralbes and Tibidabo to bohemian Gràcia, this entire northern area of the city offers stunning views and regal attractions. But what really sets this area apart from the rest of the city is its 15 parks; the best are Gaudí's stunning and imaginative Parc Güell, and the colossal natural park of Collserola, which spreads out like green baize over Tibidabo mountain. Gràcia stands out as the city's most cosmopolitan neighbourhood. Its strong political tradition and gypsy community have long drawn artists and writers to the labyrinthine streets, and it is now home to scores of innovative boutiques, bars and squares, which teem with life most nights of the week.

Parc d'Atraccions del Tibidabo

🔟 Sights & Attractions

1. Parc d'Atraccions del Tibidabo
2. Monestir de Pedralbes
3. Torre de Collserola
4. Museu del FC Barcelona & Camp Nou Stadium
5. Palau Reial de Pedralbes
6. Park Güell
7. Temple Expiatori del Sagrat Cor
8. Parc de Collserola
9. Tramvia Blau
10. Jardins del Laberint d'Horta

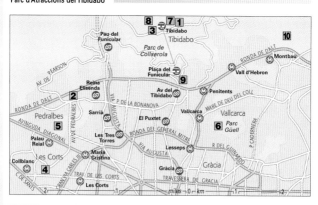

The best way to visit this area is on the Bus Turístic See p133

1 Parc d'Atraccions del Tibidabo

Take the 100-year-old funicular up to the top of Tibidabo's 517-m (1,695-ft) mountain to visit this traditional amusement park, which first opened in 1908. Although there are a couple of stomach-churning, white-knuckle rides, the real attractions are the quaint, old-fashioned ones, including a beautifully conserved carousel and a Ferris wheel. Here also is the Museu dels Autòmates *(see p41)*, with automatons, mechanical models and a scale model of the park. ⊗ Pl de Tibidabo • Map B1 • Opening times vary, call 93 211 79 42 for details • www.tibidabo.es • Adm • DA

2 Monestir de Pedralbes

Named after the Latin *petras albas*, which means white stones, this outstandingly beautiful Gothic monastery was founded by Queen Elisenda de Montcada de Piños in the early 14th century. Her alabaster tomb lies in the wall between the church and the particularly impressive three-storey Gothic cloister. An interesting glimpse of medieval life is provided by the furnished kitchens, cells, infirmary and refectory, all of which are well preserved.

⊗ C/Baixada Monestir 9 • Map A1 • Open 10am–2pm Tue–Sun • Adm; free 1st Sun of the month • DA

3 Torre de Collserola

This dynamic, slender telecommunications tower was designed by British architect Norman Foster. The needle-like upper structure rests on a concrete pillar and is anchored by 12 huge steel cables. Rising to a height of 560 m (1836 ft) above sea level, the top is reached by a glass-fronted elevator. On a clear day, you can see as far as Montserrat and the Pyrenees. ⊗ Parc de Collserola • Map B1 • Open 11am–2pm & 3:30–5pm (to 7pm weekends) daily • Adm • DA

Torre de Collserola

4 Museu del FC Barcelona & Camp Nou Stadium

Barcelona's most visited museum is a must for fans of the beautiful game. With football memorabilia of every conceivable kind, you can learn all about the club's history. Work donated by some of Catalonia's leading artists is also on display. Admission includes access to Barça's 120,000-seater stadium, an impressive monument to the city's love-affair with the game. ⊗ Entrance 9 Stadium, Av Aristides Maillol • Map A2 • Open 10am–6:30pm Mon–Sat, 10am–2:30pm Sun • Adm

Camp Nou Stadium

Gràcia

Until the end of the 19th century, Gràcia was a fiercely proud independent city. Despite locals' protests, it became part of Barcelona proper in 1898, but has always maintained a sense of separatism and has been a hotbed of political activity. It is now home to a booming cottage industry nurtured by a growing band of artisans. Don't miss the barrio's annual fiesta *(see p65)* in the second week of August.

Palau Reial de Pedralbes

The former main residence of Count Eusebi Güell was donated by the count to the Spanish royal family in 1919. Open to the public since 1937, this majestic palace now houses the Museu de Ceràmica and the Museu de les Arts Decoratives. The former has a fine collection of Catalan and Moorish ceramics, including works by Miró and Picasso; the latter has period furniture, plus a number of artifacts dating from the Middle Ages to the present day. The magnificent gardens include a fountain designed by Gaudí and some pleasant strolls. The Museu Tèxtil will move here in 2008. ◈ *Av Diagonal 686 • Map A2 • Museums open 10am–6pm Tue–Sat, 10am–3pm Sun • Adm (free 1st Sun of the month) • DA*

View, Temple Expiatori del Sagrat Cor

Parc Güell

Declared a UNESCO World Heritage Site in 1984, this heady brew of architectural wizardry includes *trencadís* tiling, a serpentine bench, fairy-tale pavilions, Gothic archways, and the columned Sala Hipóstila (originally intended as a market hall). In true Gaudí style, playfulness and symbolism pervade every aspect of the park. The Casa-Museu Gaudí, where Gaudí lived for 20 years, is dedicated to the architect's life. ◈ *C/d'Olot • Map B2 • Open 10am–dusk daily • Free* ◈ *Casa-Museu Gaudí • Map B2 • Open Oct–Mar: 10am–5:45pm; Apr–Sep: 10am–7:45pm • Adm €4*

Museu de Ceràmica, Palau Reial

Temple Expiatori del Sagrat Cor

Visible from almost anywhere in Barcelona, the Temple of the Sacred Heart was built by Enric Sagnier between 1902 and 1911. It has a dramatic sculpture of Jesus and an elaborately decorated door that verges on the psychedelic. Take the elevator up the main tower, or climb the steps to the outside terrace for breathtaking views. ◈ *Pl del Tibidabo • Map B1 • Open 10am–8pm daily (Elevator open 10:30am–2pm & 3–7pm daily) • Adm*

Parc de Collserola

Beyond the peaks of Tibidabo mountain, this 6,500-ha (16,000-acre) natural park of wild forest

Parc del Laberint d'Horta

and winding paths is an oasis of calm. It is great for hiking and biking (see p59), with sign-posted paths and nature trails. ◈ Info point: C/Església 92 • Map B1

Tramvia Blau
9 The city's blue trams, with their old-fashioned, wooden interiors are attractions in themselves. The route, from the FGC station to Plaça Doctor Andreu, passes many *Modernista* mansions to the top of Avinguda Tibidabo. ◈ Av Tibidabo • Map B1 • Trams run 10am–8pm (Oct–May 6pm) daily (mid-Sep–late June Sat, Sun & bank hols only) • Adm

Parc del Laberint d'Horta
10 In 1802, the Marquès d'Alfarràs hosted a huge party in these wonderful Neo-Classical gardens to celebrate the visit of Carles IV. Designed by Italian architect Domenico Bagotti, they incorporate a lake, a waterfall, canals and a recently restored cypress-tree maze. ◈ C/German Desvalls • Map C1 • Open 10am–dusk daily • Free (Wed & Sun), Adm (all other days)

Museu de les Arts Decoratives, Palau Reial

Exploring the Heights

Morning

Taking the northern route of the Bus Touristic (see p133) is the easiest way to negotiate the vast northern area of the city; it also gives discounts on entrance to major sights en route. Start off at Plaça de Catalunya (tickets can be bought on board) and sit on the top deck for a good view of the *Modernista* magic along Pg de Gràcia. Make the whimsical **Parc Güell** your first stop and spend the morning ambling around Gaudí's otherworldly park. Get back on the bus and continue north to the southern end of Av Tibidabo. Walk about 500 m (1600 ft) up Av Tibidabo and stop off for a leisurely lunch in the garden of the palatial **El Asador d'Aranda** (see p117).

Afternoon

After you've had your fill of fine Castilian cuisine, continue strolling up Av Tibidabo to Plaça Doctor Andreu where you can hop on the steep funicular train to go higher still to Plaça de Tibidabo. Pop into the **Parc d'Atraccions** (see p111) for a ride on the dod-gems or the Ferris wheel. Then head to the landmark **Torre de Collserola** (see p111), where a glass elevator whisks you up to an observation deck for spectacular views. Return to Plaça Doctor Andreu on the funicular and treat yourself to a *granissat* (see p43) in one of the terrace bars. Then go down Av Tibidabo on the charming **Tramvia Blau** and catch the Bus Touristic back to the city centre.

Left **Stylish accessories** Right **Clothing, Modart**

Gràcia Boutiques

Naftalina
Of all the cottage industry boutiques in Gràcia, Naftalina has the most stylish interior – befitting the equally stylish, hand-made designer clothes. Chic, elegant, understated women's wear with an emphasis on textured fabrics. ✎ C/La Perla 33

Ninas
Nina, a young American designer, sells simple, modern women's clothes made from fine fabrics. The shop is housed in a gorgeous *Modernista* building which was once a butcher's, and has a workshop at the back. ✎ C/Verdi 39

Modart
One of the first boutiques in this neighbourhood, Modart is a simple and unpretentious shop where the women's clothes speak for themselves. Garments by numerous other up-and-coming designers also feature. ✎ C/Astúries 34 • DA

José Rivero
José provides his own original in-house creations for men and women; he also sells crafted accessories, including handbags, by young local designers. ✎ C/Astúries 43

Multiart
This fabric workshop sells colourful, hand-printed textiles, bedlinen, and clothes for men and women. It also runs educational dress-making workshops. ✎ C/Sant Joaquim 23

Suite
This small boutique sells interesting and original women's and men's clothes and accessories by local designers, such as Monse Ibáñez and Dora Romero. ✎ C/Verdi 3

Camiseria Pons
One of the oldest shops in the area, this men's specialist shop sells shirts, shirts and more shirts by top Spanish and international designers, including Ralph Lauren. ✎ Gran de Gràcia 49

Gina
Cutting-edge designs – verging on punky – are the hallmark of the well-made women's clothing designed and made by Gina herself. A small and welcoming shop. ✎ C/Verdi 10 • DA

El Piano
El Piano sells elegant and stylish women's clothes with a retro flair made by Catalan designer Tina García. It also stocks clothes by other independent designers. ✎ C/Verdi 20 bis

Zucca
One of three branches in Barcelona, Zucca offers a superb range of ultra-stylish fashion accessories. The stock includes plastic flowers for your hair and stick-on navel rings. ✎ C/Torrent de l'Olla 175

Left **Sign, Cafè Salambó** Right **Tea urns, Teteria Jazmín**

TOP 10 Gràcia Cafés

1 Cafè del Sol
This café-bar is a cut above the others in the lively, bohemian Plaça del Sol. The atmosphere buzzes, the conversation inspires and the excellent coffee keeps on coming. ◈ *Pl del Sol 16 • DA*

2 Cafè Salambó
Scrumptious sandwiches and a tasty range of salads are the draw at this beautiful, wooden, trendy bar-cum-café. There are pool tables upstairs. ◈ *C/Torrijos 51 • DA*

3 Teteria Jazmín
An aromatic café that serves hundreds of different teas; the most unusual is the mint tea served with pine-kernels. Typical Morrocan dishes (*tagines* and couscous) are also available. ◈ *C/Maspons 11 • Closed Mon & 2 weeks Sep*

4 La Cafetera
Of all the cafés on Plaça de la Virreina, this one, with its outdoor terrace and tiny patio full of potted plants, is easily the most pleasant for a quiet and leisurely morning coffee and a sandwich. ◈ *Pl de la Virreina*

5 Aroma
It's always a pleasure to smell the coffee being freshly ground at this cream-walled and wood-beamed café. Hundreds of coffees to choose from, with takeaway packets available. ◈ *Travessera de Gràcia 151 • DA*

6 Vreneli
The cosy Plaça de Rius i Taulet boasts four café terraces to choose from. Vreneli is the most interesting one, with a mixture of Mexican, Swiss and Spanish fare. No alcohol is served. ◈ *Pl Rius i Taulet 11 • Closed Mon • DA*

7 Blues Cafè
The walls at this dusky, atmospheric café-bar are plastered with black-and-white photos of John Lee Hooker and Leadbelly, among others. The music, electric or acoustic, is always the blues. ◈ *C/Perla 35*

8 Cafè del Teatre
This is an ideal place to find a young, friendly crowd and good conversation. The only connection with the theatre here seems to be the velvet curtains on the sign over the door of this scruffy, but busy, café. ◈ *C/Torrijos 41*

9 Cafè de Gràcia
This airy and spacious café, with salmon walls and mirrors, is an ideal spot for a quick coffee away from the crowds. Service is speedy and a touch more formal than most places in Gràcia. ◈ *C/Gran de Gràcia 34*

10 Sureny
A new addition to this square, Sureny is simple but stylish, with a tantalizing selection of tapas and plenty of wines available by the glass. ◈ *Pl Revolució 17 • Closed Mon • DA*

Left **Mirasol** Right **Gràcia Nightlife, Plaça del Sol**

Hip Drinking Spots

Mirasol
Possibly Gràcia's most classic bar, the atmospheric Mirasol has been a bohemian hang-out for decades. In summer, there's outdoor seating on the *plaça*. ® Pl del Sol 3 • Closed Sun • DA

Universal
Open until 4:30am, Universal is a late-night, two-level bar with a spacious, airy interior. The image-concious crowd comes to flirt and dance to house (upstairs) and acid jazz (down below). There are also occasional live bands. ® C/Marià Cubí 182 • Closed Sun • Adm

Mirablau
A slightly older, well-heeled set, who adhere to the smart dress code, come to this club-bar for cocktails and amazing views of the city. ® Pl Dr Andreu

Virreina Bar
Small exhibitions by local artists, imported beers and a relaxed ambience are the draw in this old wine-cellar bar with a great location on Plaça de la Virreina. ® Pl de la Virreina 1

Casa Quimet
The "Guitar House" is always crowded and noisy. If you can play, join the enthusiasts and would-be flamenco players who pick guitars off the wall and have an impromptu jam session. Wonderful. ® C/Rambla de Prat 9 • Closed Mon–Wed & Feb & Aug

Zig Zag
The interior may be cold, but the people are far from it at Zig Zag, one of the first designer bars in town. At times, it's near to impossible to reach the dance floor. ® C/Plató 13

Otto Zutz
Barcelona's media crowd flocks to this New-York-style club to chatter in the corners upstairs and shoot pool downstairs. The huge dance floors throb with house music. ® C/Lincoln 15 • Closed Sun–Mon • Adm

Mond Bar
The comfortable sofas, low lights and innovative music policy (pop, lounge and trip-hop) make this one of the coolest hang-outs in the city. Some of Barcelona's best DJs play here. ® Pl del Sol 21

Mirabé
Next door to Mirablau and owned by the same people, Mirabé attracts younger, uptown folk for a fantastic view, eclectic pop music, a huge disco and a garden below. ® Manuel Arnús 2

Bikini
Opening from midnight onwards, this huge venue has three spaces, which offer dance and Latin music and a cocktail lounge. Regular live music includes some of the best up-and-coming acts in Europe. ® C/Deu i Mata 105 • Closed Mon • Adm • DA

 Normal closing times for bars is 2:30am, 3am weekends. Clubs open until 4:30/5am. For more on Barcelona's nightlife **See pp46–7**

Price Categories

For a three-course meal for one with half a bottle of wine (or equivalent meal), taxes and extra charges.

€	under €10
€€	€10–20
€€€	€20–30
€€€€	over €30

Interior, Flash Flash

🔟 Restaurants & Tapas Bars

1 El Asador d'Aranda
Housed in the magnificent *Modernista* Casa Roviralta, this restaurant is a magnet for business-folk. Order the delicious lamb roasted in an oak-burning oven and dine in the beautiful garden.
⊗ *Av Tibidabo 31 • 93 417 0115 • €€€€*

2 Bar-Restaurante Can Tomàs
This tapas bar, in the Sarrià neighbourhood, is an institution. It has the well-deserved reputation of making some of the best tapas in town. Particularly recommended are the *patates braves*.
⊗ *C/Major de Sarrià 49 • 93 203 10 77 • Closed Wed • No credit cards • €€*

3 A Contraluz
Uncomplicated yet innovative Mediterranean food is presented in this enchanting restaurant and its wonderful garden. The risottos are excellent, as is the hot *foie gras* with apple.
⊗ *C/Milanesat 19 • 93 203 06 58 • DA • €€€€*

4 Neichel
Top-class in every way, Neichel lures a moneyed clientele with *nouvelle cuisine* and a luscious interior. Reserve in advance.
⊗ *C/Beltrán i Rózpide 1 • 93 203 84 08 • Closed Sun & Mon • €€€€*

5 Taverna El Glop
This tavern-like local eatery serves traditional Catalan food. Its *calçots* (chargrilled, gigantic spring onions served with spicy romesco sauce) are legendary.
⊗ *C/St Lluis 24 • 93 213 70 58 • DA • €€€*

6 Can Punyetes
The ordinary becomes the exquisite at this typical Catalan restaurant. From the farmhouse bread dripping with olive oil, to the *mel i mató* (goat's cheese with honey), it's all delightful.
⊗ *C/Marià Cubí 189 • 93 200 91 59 • €€€*

7 Flash Flash
Truites (omelettes) rule here, from the classic (Spanish) to the inventive (garlic and asparagus). The owners claim to have used five million eggs in just over 30 years. ⊗ *C/Granada de Penedès 25 • 93 237 09 90 • DA • €€€*

8 La Balsa
In the quiet Bonanova district, La Balsa is a beautiful spot, with two garden terraces. Fine Basque, Catalan and Mediterranean dishes are on the menu. ⊗ *C/Infanta Isabel 4 • 93 211 50 48 • Closed Sun dinner, Mon lunch & lunch in Aug • €€€€*

9 La Venta
Take the city's only tram to the top of Av Tibidabo for traditional Catalan food washed down with bold Riojas at this terrace restaurant. ⊗ *Pl Dr Andreu • 93 212 64 55 • Closed Sun • DA • €€€€*

10 Botafumeiro
The fish tanks at this seafood restaurant are teeming with crabs and lobster destined for plates. Try the tender *pulpo Gallego* (Galician octopus). Reservations are essential. ⊗ *C/Gran de Gràcia 81 • 93 218 4230 • DA • €€€€*

Unless otherwise stated, all restaurants accept credit cards.
For more on dining and standard opening hours **See p138**

Left **Monestir de Santes Creus** Right **Cadaqués**

Beyond Barcelona

S TEEPED IN TRADITION, *with its own language and an enormous sense of pride in its separate identity, Catalonia is immensely rich in both cultural heritage and physical geography. It is no exaggeration to say that Catalonia really does have everything. To the north are the 3,000-m (9840-ft) peaks of the Pyrenees. The coastline is dotted with hundreds of beautiful sandy beaches and intimate rocky coves with crystal-clear waters. These staggering natural treasures are complemented by a wealth of fabulous churches and monasteries, many set in stunning, isolated mountain scenery. For the gourmet, the regional cuisine is particularly rewarding, while the locally-produced cava easily holds its own against its French champagne counterparts.*

Teatre-Museu Dalí

Sights & Attractions

1. Montserrat
2. Teatre-Museu Dalí, Figueres
3. Vall de Núria
4. Alt Penedès
5. Begur & Around
6. Tarragona
7. Girona
8. Empúries
9. Port Aventura
10. Costa Daurada & Sitges

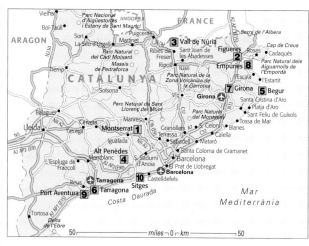

For tips on getting around Catalonia **See p132**

1 Montserrat

The dramatic mount of Montserrat, with its remote Benedictine monastery (dating from 1025), is a religious symbol and a place of pilgrimage for the Catalan people. The Basilica houses a statue of Catalonia's patron virgin, La Moreneta, also know as the "Black Virgin". Some legends date the statue to AD 50, but research

Basilica, Monestir de Montserrat

suggests it was carved in the 12th century. The monastery itself was largely destroyed in 1811 during the War of Independence, and rebuilt some 30 years later. Montserrat forms part of a ridge of mountains that rise suddenly from the plains. Take the funicular to the mountain's unspoilt peaks, where paths run alongside spectacular gorges to numerous hermitages. ◈ Tourist Info: Pl de la Creu • 93 877 77 77

2 Teatre-Museu Dalí, Figueres

Salvador Dalí was born in the town of Figueres in 1904. Paying tribute to the artist is the fantastic Teatre-Museu Dalí, which is full of his eccentric works. Housed in a former theatre, the country's second-most-visited museum (after the Prado in Madrid) provides a unique insight into the artist's extraordinary creations, from La Cesta de Pan (1926) to El Torero Alucinogeno (1970). Twenty minutes' drive away, near the beach town of Cadaqués, the Dalí connection continues. Here you can visit the Casa-Museu Salvador Dalí, the artist's summer house for nearly 60 years until his death in 1989.

◈ Pl Gala-Salvador Dalí, Figueres • 972 67 75 00 • Open Mar–Jun, Oct: 9:30am–6pm Tue–Sun; Jul–Sep: 9am–8pm daily; Nov–Feb: 10:30am–6pm Tue–Sun • Adm €10
◈ Casa-Museu Salvador Dalí, Port Lligat • 972 25 10 15 • Closed early Jan to mid-Mar • Guided visits only, Tue–Sun by reservation • Adm €10

3 Vall de Núria

This enchanting Pyrenean hideaway, surrounded by crests reaching as high as 3,000-m (9,840-ft), is a ski resort in winter and a green, peaceful oasis attracting hikers and nature-lovers in summer. The mountain resort centres on a tiny religious sanctuary and has a youth hostel and apartments for rent. The beautiful valley is only accessible via a silent cog railway, which trundles above the clouds through breathtaking mountain scenery.
◈ Tourist Info: Railway Station, Vall de Núria • 972 73 20 20 • Rack railway train from Ribes de Freser, 10 km N Ripoll

Rainy Taxi, Teatre-Museu Dalí

 Anywhere in Catalonia can be reached by car from Barcelona in less than three hours.

Alt Penedès

Catalonia's most famous wine region is the *cava*-producing area of the Penedès. The *cava* brands of Cordoníu and Freixenet have become household names worldwide. Many of the area's wineries and bodegas are open to the public. One of the most spectacular is the Cordoníu bodega, housed in a *Modernista* building designed by Puig i Cadafalch, with a phenomenal 26 km (16 miles) of cellars on five floors. ❧ *Tourist Info: C/Cort 14, Vilafranca del Penedès • 93 818 12 54 • The tourist office has details on all winery visits in the region, including the Cordoníu winery*

Begur & Around

The elegant hilltop town of Begur, with its ruined 14th-century castle, looks down on the nature reserve of Aiguamolla and some of the prettiest coves on the Costa Brava. The town's population quadruples in summer as visitors make this their base for exploring nearby beaches and small, isolated coves. Many of the area's beaches stage jazz concerts throughout the summer. This is perhaps the best stretch of coastline in Catalonia. ❧ *Tourist Info: Av Onze de Setembre 5 • 972 62 45 20*

Tarragona

Entering the city of Tarragona, past the oil refineries and its huge industrial port, it's hard to envisage the astounding archaeological treasures that await. Once the capital of Roman Catalonia, the city's main attractions today are from this era. Highlights include an impressive amphitheatre and the well-kept Roman

Riu Onyar, Girona

walls that lead past the Museu Nacional Arqueològic and the Torre de Pilatos, a tower where Christians were supposedly imprisoned before being thrown to the lions. Also in Tarragona is the Catedral de Santa Tecla *(see p124)*. ❧ *Tourist Info: C/Fortuny 4 • 977 23 34 15*

Girona

Said to have the highest living standards in Catalonia, Girona is a pleasant town surrounded by lush green hills. Hidden away in the old town, the atmospheric Jewish quarter (known as El Call) is one of the best-preserved medieval enclaves in Europe. Girona's cathedral is a must *(see p124)*. ❧ *Tourist Info: Rambla de la Llibertat 1 • 972 22 65 75*

Codorníu *cava*

Empúries

After Tarragona, Empúries is Catalonia's second most important Roman site. Occupying an impressive position by the sea, it includes more than 40 hectares (99 acres) scattered with Greek and Roman ruins, the highlights of which are the remains of a market street, various temples and part of a Roman amphitheatre. Coupled with lovely nearby beaches, it's an ideal spot for those looking to mix a bit of history with a dip in the sea. ⚲ *Empúries • 972 77 02 08 • Open Jun–Sep: 10am–8pm daily; Oct–May: 10am–6pm daily • Adm*

Port Aventura

9 Universal Studios' theme park is divided up into five areas: China, Far West, Mediterranean, Polynesia and Mexico, each offering rides and attractions. Thrill-junkies will appreciate one of Europe's biggest roller coasters, Dragon Kahn (China). There are also shows, and the entire experience is like being on a film set. ⚲ *Av Pere Molas, Vila-seca, Tarragona • 902 20 22 20 • Open mid-Mar–Oct daily, call for seasonal hours • Adm • DA*

Costa Daurada & Sitges

10 With its wide sandy beaches and shallow waters, the Costa Daurada differs from the northern Catalonian coastline. The sleepy town of Torredembarra is a pleasant and rarely busy family resort, but the jewel in the crown is undoubtedly Sitges. It's the summer home to Barcelona's chic crowd, as well as being a popular gay resort *(see p49)*. All this gives it a cosmopolitan, frenetic feel, but the town never reaches the tacky excesses of some of the Costa Brava's resorts. ⚲ *Tourist Info: C/Sínia Morera • 902 10 34 28*

Waterfront, Sitges

A Scenic Drive

Morning

🕐 From Barcelona take the AP7 motorway until exit 4, then take the C260 to Cadaqués. The journey should take about two and a half hours in all. Just before dropping down to the town, stop at the viewpoint and take in the azure coastline and the whitewashed houses of this former fishing village. Once in **Cadaqués**, now one of Catalonia's trendiest beach towns, wander the quaint boutique-filled streets. After a splash in the sea and a coffee on one of the chic terrace cafés, take the road leaving Port Lligat and head for the **Cap de Creus** *(see p125)* lighthouse. Drive through the desolately beautiful landscape of this rocky headland before doubling back and heading off to Port de la Selva. The road twists and winds interminably, but the picture-perfect scenery will leave you speechless.

Afternoon

Stop in the tiny, mountain-enclosed Port de la Selva for an excellent seafood lunch at the Cala Herminda. Then drive to the neighbouring village of Selva del Mar with its tiny river and have a post-prandial coffee on the terrace of the Bar Stop before continuing up to the **Monestir Sant Pere de Rodes** *(see p124)*. You'll be tempted to stop several times on the way up to take in the views. Don't, because the best is to be had from the monastery, which offers an incredible sweeping vista of the whole area. There are plenty of well-signposted walks around the mountain top here and it is worth staying put to see the sun set slowly over the bay.

Beyond Barcelona

Following pages **Inner Courtyard, Monestir de Montserrat**

Left **Chapterhouse detail, Monestir de Santes Creus** Right **Monestir de Poblet**

Churches & Monasteries

Monestir de Montserrat
Catalonia's holiest place is the region's most visited monastery. It boasts some Romanesque art and a statue of the "Black Virgin". *See p119.* ❧ *Montserrat • 93 877 77 77 • Adm • DA to Basilica*

Monestir de Poblet
This busy, working monastery contains the Gothic Capella de Sant Jordi, a Romanesque church, and the Porta Daurada, a doorway that was gilded for Felipe II's visit in 1564. ❧ *off N240, 10 km W of Montblanc • 977 870 254 • Adm*

Monestir de Ripoll
The west portal of this monastery (879) has reputedly the finest Romanesque carvings in Spain. Of the original buildings, only the doorway and cloister remain. ❧ *Ripoll • 972 70 23 51 • Adm*

Monestir de Santes Creus
The cloister at this Gothic treasure (1150) is notable for the beautifully sculpted capitals by English artist Reinard Funoll.
❧ *Santes Creus, 25 km NW of Montblanc • 977 63 83 29 • Closed Mon • Adm • Tue free*

Monestir de Sant Pere de Rodes
The dilapidated charm of this UNESCO World Heritage Site may have dwindled since its face-lift, but nothing detracts from the views it offers over Cap de Creus and Port de la Selva. ❧ *22 km E of Figueres • 972 38 75 59 • Closed Mon • Adm*

Sant Climent i Santa Maria de Taüll
These two churches are perfect examples of the Romanesque churches that pepper the Pyrenees. Dating from 1123, most of the original frescoes are now in the MNAC in Barcelona *(see pp18–19)*. ❧ *138 km N of Lleida • 973 69 40 00*

Catedral de La Seu d'Urgell
Dating from around 1040, this cathedral is one of the most elegant in Catalonia. ❧ *La Seu d'Urgell • 973 35 15 11 • Free • DA*

Catedral de Santa Maria
This cathedral is remarkable for possessing the widest Gothic nave anywhere in Europe and the second widest of any type after the Basilica in the Vatican. ❧ *Old Town, Girona • 972 21 44 26 • Adm €4 • Sun free*

Catedral de Santa Tecla
At 104-m (340-ft) long, Tarragona's cathedral is the largest in the region. Its architecture is a mixture of Gothic and Romanesque, and it is crowned by a huge octagonal bell tower. ❧ *Old Town, Tarragona • 977 25 07 95 • Closed Sun except for 11am mass • Adm*

Sant Joan de les Abadesses
This pretty French Romanesque-style monastery in the Pyrenees harbours a prestigious collection of Romanesque sculpture. ❧ *Sant Joan de les Abadesses • 972 72 05 99 • www.santjoandelesabadesses.com • Adm*

 Usual opening hours for monasteries and churches are 10am–1pm & 3–7pm Mon–Sat, 10am–1pm Sun. Call to confirm seasonal times.

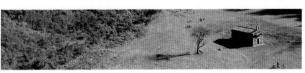

Parc Natural de la Zona Volcànica de la Garrotxa

TOP 10 National Parks & Nature Reserves

1 Parc Nacional d'Aigüestortes i Estany de Sant Maurici

The magnificent peaks of Catalonia's only national park are accessible from the resort of Espot. You'll find ponds and lakes 2,000 m (6,560 ft) up. ◈ *148 km N of Lleida*

2 Delta de l'Ebre

This giant delta is a patchwork of paddy fields. The wide expanse of the River Ebre is a nature reserve for migratory birds and has scores of bird-watching stations. ◈ *28 km SE of Tortosa*

3 Parc Natural de la Zona Volcànica de la Garrotxa

It is 10,000 years since La Garrotxa last erupted and the volcanoes are long since extinct. The largest crater is the Santa Margalida, at 500 m (1,640 ft) wide. It is magical here in spring when thousands of butterflies emerge. ◈ *40 km NW of Girona*

4 Cap de Creus

As the Pyrenees tumble into the Mediterranean, they create a rocky headland, which juts out 10 km (6.25 miles). It forms Catalonia's most easterly point and offers spectacular views of the craggy coastline. ◈ *36 km E of Figueres*

5 Parc Natural del Cadí-Moixeró

Covered in a carpet of conifers and oaks, this mountain range has surprisingly lush vegetation. Several peaks are over 2,000 m (6,560 ft) high. ◈ *20 km E of La Seu d'Urgell*

6 Parc Natural del Montseny

Forming Catalonia's most accessible natural park, these woodland hills are well-equipped for walkers and mountain bikers, with a huge network of trails. Climb the well-signposted and popular Turó de l'Home, which is the highest peak. ◈ *48 km NW of Barcelona*

7 Massís de Pedraforca

A nature reserve surrounds this huge outcrop of mountains, a favourite of rock climbers with peaks rising to 2,500 m (8,200 ft). ◈ *64 km N of Manresa*

8 Serra de l'Albera

On the eastern part of the border between Spain and France, the tree-covered slopes of Albera are speckled with interesting ruins. ◈ *15 km N of Figueres*

9 Parc Natural dels Aiguamolls de l'Empordà

This nature reserve hides birdwatching towers. Those in the Laguna de Vilalt and La Bassa de Gall Mari allow bird-lovers to observe herons, moorhens and other bird species nesting in spring. ◈ *15 km E of Figueres*

10 Parc Natural de Sant Llorenç del Munt

Surrounded by industry and within easy reach of Barcelona, this is a surprisingly untamed park inhabited by large numbers of wild boar. Walk up Cerro de la Mola to see the Romanesque monastery. ◈ *12 km E of Manresa*

Rafting, La Noguera Pallaresa

🔟 Outdoor Activities

Rafting & Kayaking
One of Europe's best rivers for white-water sports is La Noguera Pallaresa in the Pyrenees. Late spring is the best time to go, as the mountain snow thaws. ✎ *Yeti Emotions: • Llavorsi, 14 km N of Sort • 973 62 22 01 • www.yetiemotions.com*

Scuba Diving
The beautiful Reserva Natural de les Illes Medes, with its thousands of species and coral reefs, is a haven for divers. Glass-bottomed boats cater to non-divers. ✎ *López Bender, Port Alegre 1, Ampuriabrava • 972 45 02 41 • www.lopez-bender-sub.com*

Watersports & Sailing
Good sailing can be found in Sitges, along with yachts for rent, classes for the novice, canoeing and windsurfing. ✎ *Club de Mar Sitges, Pg Marítim, Sitges • 93 894 09 05 • www.clubdemardesitges.com*

Skiing
La Molina is the most accessible ski-resort from Barcelona, but Baqueira-Beret is where the jet-set goes. Both offer all levels of skiing (including off-piste) from December. ✎ *La Molina, 25 km S of Puigcerdà • 972 89 20 33 • www.lamolina.com Baqueira-Beret, 14 km E of Vielha • 973 63 90 00 (snow reports: 973 63 90 25) • www.baqueira.es*

Golf
The Costa Brava is one of Europe's top golf destinations; the best courses are around Platja

d'Aro. ✎ *Santa Cristina d'Aro • 972 83 71 50 ✎ Platja d'Aro • 972 82 69 00*

Horse Riding
Montseny national park *(see p125)* is ideal for horse riding, with a number of centres. ✎ *Can Marc, 6 km W of Sant Celoni • 938 48 27 13*

Ballooning
A balloon journey over the volcanic area of Osona is an unbeatable way to get a bird's-eye view of Catalonia. ✎ *Baló Tour, Vic • 93 414 47 74 • www.balotour.com*

Boat trips
Take a picturesque cruise from Calella and Blanes to Tossa de Mar, stopping at the old town and the castle of Tossa de Mar. ✎ *Dofi Jet Boats, Blanes • 972 35 20 21 www.dofijetboats.com • boats every hour daily from Blanes (twice daily from Calella) • Closed Nov–Feb*

Windsurfing, Rowing & Golf
Used for rowing competitions in the 1992 Olympics, the huge Canal Olímpic is now a leisure complex offering a host of activities. ✎ *Canal Olímpic • Av Canal Olímpic, Castelldefels • 93 636 28 96*

Foraging for Mushrooms
From late September to late October, thousands of Catalans flock to the hills in search of the highly prized *rovelló*. There are also poisonous varieties, so amateurs should get a guide through the Diputació de Barcelona.

Diputació de Barcelona has information on activities in Catalonia, from gastro tours to guided walks. Check www.turismetotal.org

Price Categories

For a three-course meal for one with half a bottle of wine (or equivalent meal), taxes and extra charges.

€ under €10
€€ €10–20
€€€ €20–30
€€€€ over €30

Anchovy tapas, El Pescadors

Places to Eat

1 El Bulli
A once-in-a-lifetime experience. Extraordinary creations by the three-Michelin-star chef Ferran Adrià such as wild mushrooms in test tubes. Book months in advance (via their website). *Cala de Montjoi, Roses • 972 150 457 • Closed Oct–Mar • www.elbulli.com • €€€€*

2 El Racó de Can Fabes
The trad French-Catalan food at this three-Michelin-star country-house restaurant includes duck in blood with cep mushrooms. *Sant Joan 6, Sant Celoni, Montseny • 93 867 28 51 • www.canfabes.com • Closed Sun eve & Mon • €€€€*

3 La Torre del Remei
A *Modernista* palace provides an elegant setting for wonderfully presented Catalan food. The game dishes are sublime. *Camí Reial, Bolvir, Cerdanya, 3 km SW of Puigcerdà • 972 14 01 82 • DA • €€€€*

4 El Mirador de les Caves
This restaurant is set in a castle overlooking Catalonia's wine country. Traditional cuisine is complemented by bottles of local wine and *cava*. *Els Casots, 4 km S of Sant Sadurní d'Anoia • 93 899 31 78 • Closed Sun eve & Mon eve • €€€€*

5 Fonda Europa
Established over 150 years ago, Fonda Europa was the first in a line of successful Catalan restaurants. Ample portions include pig's trotters. *Anselm Clavé 1, Granollers • 93 870 0312 • €€€*

6 Mare Nostrum
The seafood at this family restaurant, with its splendid terrace, includes typical paella and *sípia a la planxa* (grilled cuttlefish). *Pg de la Ribera 60, Sitges • 93 894 33 93 • Closed Wed, & 15 Dec–1 Feb • DA • €€€€*

7 Parador de Aiguablava
On a rocky outcrop, this restaurant has phenomenal service and stunning views over Aiguablava cove. The food is good, if a bit predictable. Rooms are available. *Cala Aiguablava, 4 km S of Begúr • 972 62 21 62 • €€€*

8 Els Pescadors
"The Fishermen", a traditional *Empordà*-style restaurant, offers local specialities, including an array of blue fish dishes. *Port d'en Perris 3, l'Escala • 972 77 07 28 • www.pescadors.com • Closed Sun eve (winter), Thu & Nov • €€€€*

9 Cal Ros
Girona's oldest restaurant is also one of its most popular. Wild mushrooms used in traditional Catalan meat dishes add a magical touch. *Cort Reial 9, Girona • 972 21 91 76 • Closed Sun eve & Mon • €€€€*

10 Can Boix
Foodies come to Boix (in Cadí-Moixeró natural park) for country cooking including crabs' legs, lobster and many meat dishes. *Cadí-Moixeró, Martinet • 973 51 50 50 • Closed Sun eve & Mon • €€€€*

Unless otherwise stated, all restaurants accept credit cards. For more on dining and standard opening hours See p138

STREETSMART

BARCELONA'S TOP 10

Left **Airport sign** Right **Iberia logo**

🔟 Tips on Getting To Barcelona

1 By Air
British Airways, Iberia and easyJet offer direct flights from the UK to Barcelona. From the US, Delta and Continental fly direct from the east coast, but flights from the west coast usually involve one stopover. Qantas flies from Australia and New Zealand to Barcelona via a series of stopovers. ✪ British Airways: 902 13 21 32 • www.britishairways.com ✪ Iberia: 902 40 05 00 • www.iberia.es ✪ easyJet: • 902 29 99 92 • www.easyjet.com ✪ Delta: 90 111 69 46 • www.delta.com ✪ Continental: www.continental.com

2 Barcelona Airport
Prat de Llobregat airport's two adjoining terminals are 12 km (7 miles) south of the city centre. ✪ 902 40 47 04 • www.aena.es

3 From the Airport
One of the most convenient ways from the airport to the city centre is by Aerobús, which depart every 6 minutes from 5:30am to 1am, and make various stops, terminating at Plaça de Catalunya. RENFE trains leave the airport every 30 minutes, stopping at Estació de Sants, Passeig de Gràcia and Estació de França; all link up with the metro. A taxi from the airport into the city centre costs €20–€25. ✪ Aerobús: 93 415 60 20 ✪ RENFE: 902 24 02 02

4 By Train
Trains run throughout Spain and the rest of Europe from Estació de Sants and Estació de França. Both stations have lockers, ATMs and bureaux de change. RENFE is Spain's national train company. ✪ Estació de França: • Av Marqués de l'Argentera • Map Q5 ✪ Estació de Sants: • Pl dels Països Catalans • Off map ✪ RENFE: 902 24 02 02 (24 hours) • www.renfe.es

5 By Bus
Both Eurolines and Linebús serve Barcelona from numerous European cities, including Rome, Paris and London. Buses usually operate from Barcelona's main bus station, Estació del Nord, and also from Estació de Sants. ✪ Estació del Nord: • C/Ali Bei 80 • Map R2 • 90 226 06 06 ✪ Eurolines: 90 240 50 40 ✪ Linebús: 90 233 55 33

6 By Car
Barcelona is well linked to the rest of Europe and Spain by a number of autopistes (toll highways) and toll-free roads. The tolled AP7 runs between Barcelona and the border of France.

7 Domestic travel
The city is connected to the rest of Spain by train, bus and plane. Iberia and its low-cost airline Click fly to and from many domestic destinations and offer a shuttle service between Madrid and Barcelona with up to 30 flights a day. Spanair, Vueling and Air Europa serve Barcelona from the rest of Spain. RENFE and several bus companies link Barcelona to most of Spain's major cities. ✪ Spanair: 902 13 14 15 • www.spanair.es ✪ Air Europa: 902 40 15 01 • www.air-europa.com ✪ Vueling: www.vueling.com

8 Cheap Travel
Book long before your departure date to cut costs. If you're flexible and open to stopovers, you're likely to find better deals. The internet is great for cheap fares (try www.travelocity.com or www.cheaptickets.com). Many airlines offer special discounts if you purchase online.

9 Planning
Citizens from the US, Canada, the UK, Ireland, Australia and New Zealand need a valid passport. For non-EU citizens, a visa is required if you intend to stay in Spain for longer than three months. If you're taking any kind of medication, bring your prescription.

10 When to Visit
If you're in search of sun, visit Barcelona during the blazing months of July or August. To avoid the crowds, however, the best time is before or after the peak summer months, in May or October.

130 *Share your travel recommendations on traveldk.com*

Streetsmart

Left **Metro sign** Centre **Barcelona taxi** Right **Metro mural**

🔟 Tips on Getting Around Barcelona

1 Metro
Barcelona's five-line metro system is convenient, fast, easy to use and extensive. The metro stays open until 2am at weekends. 🕾 *93 318 70 74* • *www.tmb.net* • *Open 5am–midnight Mon–Thu, 5am–2am Fri–Sat, 6am–midnight Sun*

2 FGC
The FGC (Ferrocarrils de la Generalitat de Catalunya) is the city's commuter rail system, serving northern and eastern Barcelona. The FGC shares several key stations with the metro, including Plaça de Catalunya and Plaça d'Espanya, and has the same prices and similar hours. 🕾 *93 205 15 15* • *www.fgc.es* • *Open 5am–midnight Mon–Thu, 5am–2am Fri–Sat, 6am–midnight Sun*

3 Bus
Barcelona's bus system covers the entire city. Bus stops are clearly marked and buses have their destinations on the front. For information on routes and schedules call 010 or pick up a bus guide from tourist offices. 🕾 *93 318 70 74* • *www.tmb.net* • *6am–10pm daily*

4 Nightbus
There are about 17 Nitbús (nightbus) routes across the city, many of which pass through Plaça de Catalunya. 🕾 *93 318 70 74* • *www.tmb.net*

5 Tickets & Passes
A single fare on the metro, FGC, bus or night-bus costs €1.30. The T-10 personal ticket costs €7 and permits 10 journeys on metro, FGC and bus, providing the total journey is completed within 1 hour 15 minutes. Also available are one-, two-, three-, four- and five-day passes, which provide unlimited travel on public transport. Tickets are available from attendants and machines at all metro stations.

6 Taxi
Hail a yellow-and-black taxi on any major street in town; a green light on the roof indicates that one is free. For two or more passengers, taxis are almost as cheap as the metro for short hops. A minimum fare applies. 🕾 *Taxi Radio: 93 303 30 33* 🕾 *Barna Taxi: 93 357 77 55*

7 On Foot
Barcelona is extremely compact and most areas are best negotiated on foot, especially the old town and Gràcia, where a leisurely stroll is the only way to soak up the architectural and cutural riches. Barcelona's waterfront, from the Port Vell to the Port Olímpic, is also made for walking. *See pp58–9.*

8 By Bicycle
Pedalling around the port, Barri Gòtic or Parc de la Ciutadella is a refreshing alternative to walking. There are over 70 km (43 miles) of bike lanes throughout the city, outlined on maps available from the tourist office and bike rental shops. Bikes are available to rent daily from Budget Bikes or CicloBus. 🕾 *Budget Bikes: 93 304 18 85* 🕾 *CicloBus: 93 285 38 32*

9 Transport for the Disabled
The airport bus is accessible to wheelchair users, as is Line 2 of the metro, some city buses, a few FGC stations and all nightbuses. Taxi Amic has cars and vans dedicated to wheelchair users – give advance notice. For information on transport for the disabled, call Informació Transport Adaptat. For information on specific routes, call 010 or TMB, Barcelona's bus and metro system. 🕾 *Taxi Amic: 93 420 80 88* • *Informació Transport Adaptat: 93 486 07 52* 🕾 *TMB: 93 318 70 74*

10 Getting Around in a Wheelchair
Barcelona's Institut Municipal de Persones amb Disminució *(see p134)* has developed a detailed computer database that charts all the streets accessible to wheelchair users. Call 010, give your departure point and destination, and they'll advise you of a route and places accessible en route.

Left **RENFE train ticket** Centre **Road sign** Right **RENFE sign**

🔟 Ways to Explore Catalonia

By Train

RENFE operates lines out of Barcelona in all directions, making it easy to escape the city. Most regional trains leave from Estació de Sants *(see p130)* and Estació Passeig de Gràcia. Call the RENFE information line for destinations and schedules.
⊗ *Estació Passeig de Gràcia • Pg de Gràcia • Map E2*
⊗ *RENFE • 902 24 02 02*

By Bus

Numerous regional bus companies operate all over Catalonia. Most depart from Estació del Nord – call the station for more information. ⊗ *Estació del Nord: C/Ali Bei 80 • Map R2 • 90 226 06 06 • www.barcelonanord.com*

By Car

A car is essential if you wish to explore off the beaten track, particularly in the Pyrenees and the Catalonian heartland. There are many car rental companies, including all the big names (Avis, Budget, Hertz), all of which have offices at the airport. Prices range from €240–420 for a medium-sized car for a week. To rent a car, you should be over 25, and have a valid driver's licence, a credit card and a passport. Booking your rental car from abroad or on-line is often cheaper. ⊗ *Avis: 90 218 08 54 • www.avis.com*
⊗ *Budget: 93 298 35 00 • www.budget.com*

⊗ *Hertz: 91 372 93 00 • www.hertz.com*

By Bike

Mountain bikers will find a wealth of rugged terrain in the Pyrenees. The Turisme de Catalunya has maps and brochures as well as a good website showing regional bike routes. Club Element leads mountain-bike tours through the lush Cerdanya Valley and along the Costa Brava. ⊗ *Club Element • Pl Lesseps 33 • 90 219 04 15*

Sea Cruises

"Sightsea" off the Costa Brava aboard glass-bottomed boats and other sea cruisers. L'Aventura del Nautilus conducts coastal sea cruises from L'Estartit to the Medes Islands off the Costa Brava. Excursiones Marítimas plies the Mediterranean from Calella and Blanes to Tossa de Mar, stopping at lovely coves along the way.
⊗ *L'Aventura del Nautilus: L'Estartit, 100km N of Barcelona • 972 75 14 89*
⊗ *Dofi Jet Boats: Calella, 40km N of Barcelona; Blanes, 60 km N of Barcelona • 972 35 20 21*

Bus Tours

Discover Catalonia on organized bus tours, which include trips to the Monestir de Montserrat, Girona, the Teatre-Museu Dalí in Figueres and the Costa Brava. Also offered is a one-day tour that visits Montserrat and Barcelona's *Modernista*

marvels. Bus tours are organized by Julià and Pullmantur. ⊗ *Julià Tours: Ronda Universitat 5 • 93 317 64 54 • www.julia tours.es* ⊗ *Pullmantur: Gran Via de les Corts Catalanes 645 • 93 317 12 97*

Main Roads

The new numbers for many roads in Catalonia that were issued in 2001 are now all that appear on signs. The old names have been phased out.

Avoiding Traffic

The best time to get out of town is in the late morning. Avoid long holiday weekends *(pont)* and Friday evenings, when traffic is always heavy. Since most Spanish take their holidays in August, motorways are particularly busy around this period.

Tips for Families

RENFE offers a 40 per cent discount for children aged four to 11. Enquire when booking tickets.

Turisme de Catalunya

This well-stocked tourist office offers plenty of material on Catalonia, from maps to information on outdoor sports and festival listings. Changing exhibits on the region are also on display.
⊗ *Palau Robert, Pg de Gràcia 105 • Map E2 • 012 • www.gencat.es/probert • Open 10am–7pm Mon–Sat, 10am–2:30pm Sun*

Streetsmart

132 *For recommended trips out of Barcelona See pp118–127*

Left **Tren Turistic** Right **Bus Turistic, Plaça de Catalunya**

🔟 Tours & Trips

① Bus Tours

The open-topped Bus Turístic is a grand way to experience the city's sights and sounds. The red route explores northern Barcelona; the blue route takes in the southern area. You can hop on and off as many times as you like. Discounts to sights and shops are included. ⊗ *Depart from Pl de Catalunya • Every 5–25 mins 9am–7pm (8pm Apr–Oct) daily • Purchase on the bus, at tourist offices and at Estació de Sants*

② Walking Tours

The tourist office *(see p134)* organizes reasonably-priced guided walks from the main office in Plaça de Catalunya – they explore the Roman and medieval history of the Barri Gòtic. The Travel Bar *(see p134)* also conducts lively walking tours.

③ La Ruta Modernista

Guided tours in English of the facades of the Mansana de la Discòrdia. Tickets offer a map and 50 per cent discount on some admission fees. For tickets, tours and information, visit the Centre del Modernisme at the Tourist Information Office in Plaça Catalunya. ⊗ *010*

④ Boat Tours

See the city from the sea on one of Les Golondrines' sightseeing boats. Trips lasting 35 minutes depart every half-hour; longer tours are available on a catamaran with an underwater view. The Voyages Orsom sailing catamaran departs from Portal de la Pau for a leisurely glide through the port. ⊗ *Les Golondrines: Portal de la Pau • 93 442 31 06 • www.lasgolondrinas.com* ⊗ *Orsom Catamaran: • Portal de la Pau • 93 441 05 37 • www.barcelona-orsom. com*

⑤ Cable Cars

Cable cars *(telefèric)* depart from Montjuïc (Miramar station), Torre de Jaume I and Torre de Sant Sebastià, yielding stunning views of the city. ⊗ *93 441 48 20*

⑥ Night Kayaking

Kayak under the stars off Barcelona's shores on a summer's night – with a beer and *pica pica* (snack) en route. Nàutica Base arranges various outdoor water activities and provides all the necessary equipment and insurance. After kayaking, go back to base for a barbecue, cocktails and ambient, DJ-spun music. ⊗ *Base Nàutica Municipal, Platja Mar Bella • 93 221 04 32 • Jun–Sep: 9pm Thu–Sat*

⑦ Coach & Car Tours

See Barcelona's major sights and neighbourhoods on a guided coach tour organized by Julià or Pullmantur Tours.

Also offered are nighttime tours (Thu–Sat), with a stop for tapas followed by a flamenco or other music show. Live Barcelona organizes group guided tours in a Mercedes van (for up to seven people). ⊗ *Julià Tours • 93 317 64 54 • www.juliatours.es* ⊗ *Pullmantur • 93 318 02 41* ⊗ *Live Barcelona Car Tours • 93 632 72 59 • www.livebarcelona.com*

⑧ Bike Tours

Whiz about the old town and the Parc de la Ciutadella on group bike tours organized by bike rental shop Un Cotxe Menys ("One Car Less"). Barcelona by Bike also runs bike tours in English. ⊗ *Un Cotxe Menys, C/Esparteria 3 • 93 268 21 05* ⊗ *Barcelona by Bike: 93 268 81 07 • Open all year • www. barcelonabybike.com*

⑨ Horse-drawn Carriages

It may be a tourist trap, but riding up La Rambla on a horse and carriage can raise a smile, especially for kids. ⊗ *Depart from Pl de Portal de la Pau • 93 421 15 49*

⑩ Tren Turístic

Explore Montjuïc on this sightseeing train, which departs from Plaça d'Espanya and climbs past all the main sights. Get on and off as you wish. ⊗ *93 415 60 20 • Open Apr–Oct*

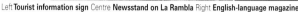

Left **Tourist information sign** Centre **Newsstand on La Rambla** Right **English-language magazine**

⑩ Sources of Information

1 Tourist Information

Multilingual staff give out free maps and information at Barcelona's main tourist office in Plaça de Catalunya. They also have a hotel booking service, a bureau de change, internet access and a souvenir shop. Other offices are located in Estació de Sants and on Plaça de Sant Jaume. For information on the rest of Catalonia, visit the Turisme de Catalunya (see p132). For information over the phone on everything from museum opening hours to bus routes, call 010 or the Turisme de Barcelona's information line. ❧ Turisme de Barcelona, Pl de Catalunya 1 • Map M1 • www.barcelonaturisme.com • 93 285 38 34 • Open 9am–9pm daily

2 Information Officers

In summer red-jacketed tourist information officers roam the city's busiest areas giving out maps and advice; and there is also an information point in Las Ramblas.

3 Magazines

The indispensable weekly Guía del Ocio covers the city's nightlife (music, theatre, dance and film). It has extensive listings of restaurants and nightlife and is available from all newsstands. Barcelona Metropolitan (free) is the city's leading English-language monthly magazine, featuring culture, the

arts and restaurant and nightlife listings. Broadsheet is another English-language monthly. b-guided gives the latest on trendy places to shop, eat and drink – in English and Spanish.

4 Consulates

Various nations have consulates in Barcelona. ❧ UK: Av Diagonal 477 • 93 366 62 00 ❧ US: Pg Reina Elisenda 23 • 93 280 22 27 ❧ Australia: Pl Gala Placidia 1–3, 1st floor • 93 490 90 13 ❧ New Zealand: Travessera de Gràcia 64 • 93 209 03 99 ❧ Canada: C/Elisenda de Pinós 10 • 93 204 27 00 ❧ Ireland: Gran Via Carles III 94 • 93 491 50 21

5 Institut de Cultura de Barcelona

Get the lowdown on cultural and arts events among others, from the Institut de Cultura in the Palau de la Virreina (see p13). ❧ La Rambla 99 • 93 301 77 75 • Open 11am–8pm Mon–Sat, 11am–2:30pm Sun

6 Websites

Numerous websites cover Barcelona, including the official tourist office site (www.barcelona turisme.com). The in-depth www.bcn.es is another excellent source. The website of Turisme de Catalunya (www.gencat.es/probert) has extensive coverage of Catalonia.

7 TravelBar

This friendly bar, with internet access and

amiable staff, is a good source of information. The bar hosts guided walking (see p133) and bike tours, "intercambio" nights to practise your Spanish, and a popular bar crawl to the best bars of the old town. ❧ C/Boqueria 27 • 93 342 52 52

8 University Bulletins

If you're after cheap, short-term accommodation or if you're looking to practise your Spanish, peruse the university notice boards posted around the building's cloisters. ❧ Gran Via de les Corts Catalanes • 93 403 54 17

9 Libraries & British Institute

The city's main library is the Biblioteca de Catalunya; bring your passport to apply for a one-day pass. The Institut Britànic houses a library of English books and newspapers. ❧ Biblioteca de Catalunya: C/Hospital 56 Institut Britànic: C/Amigó 83 • Closed Aug

10 Disabled Travellers

Disabled access in Barcelona is limited – especially in old buildings. The Institut Municipal de Persones amb Disminució provides a list of places with wheelchair access and gives advice on getting around. ❧ Av Diagonal 233 • 93 413 27 75

Streetsmart

Left **Postage stamp** Centre **Telephone** Right **Mailbox**

🔟 Communication Tips

1 Public Phones

There are public phones (*cabines*) throughout the city. Use coins or a phonecard.

2 Phonecards

Purchase a phonecard from a newsstand, phone centre or tobacco shop (*estanc*). The Telefónica phonecard comes in denominations of €6 and €12. Other phonecards (BT, Fortune) for international calls are also available and tend to offer cheaper calls.

3 Long-Distance Calls

To make an international call, dial 00 followed by the country code (UK: 44; US/Canada: 1; Australia: 61; New Zealand: 64), the area code and the phone number. To call Spain from abroad, dial the international access code then 34 for Spain plus the full phone number. To make a collect call, or to pay by credit card or your calling card, dial the international operator (9009900) plus the country code. For operator assistance in making international calls from Spain, dial 1008 for EU countries and 1005 for all others. For international information and directory enquiries, dial 11825.

4 Local & Regional Calls

The cost of a local call from a phone booth to a land line is generally about 20 cents. Barcelona phone numbers all begin with the code 93; the rest of Catalonia is divided up into the provinces of Lleida (973), Girona (972) and Tarragona (977). For operator assistance, dial 11818.

5 Phone Centres

Phone centres (*locutoris*) provide a more comfortable – and usually cheaper – alternative to public pay phones. Phones are hooked up to a digital display showing the cost, which is paid at the end. Note that the more central the location, the more expensive the call. Prices do not vary dramatically, but Telecomunicaciones del Caribe offers some of the best prices in the city centre. 🕲 *Telecomunicaciones del Caribe: C/Xuclà 16*

6 Post

Post offices (*correus*) are usually open 8:30am–8:30pm Mon–Fri and 9:30am–1pm Sat, though hours may vary slightly. Barcelona's main post office is open longer hours. It also offers a range of services, including fax and express mail services (*urgente*). The city's mailboxes are bright yellow, generally with one slot for *ciutat* (city) and one for *altres destinacions* (other destinations). 🕲 *Main Post Office: Pl Antoni López*

• *Open 8:30am–10pm Mon–Sat, noon–10pm Sun*

7 Poste Restante

You can receive mail at any post office, but it's safest to have it sent to the main one. Bring your passport (or a copy of it) to collect mail. 🕲 *Address letters to: Lista de Correos, 08070, Barcelona, Spain*

8 Internet Access

Internet centres are dotted all over Barcelona, many around Plaça de Catalunya and La Rambla. Most are open until 11pm, sometimes midnight. For 24-hour internet access, head to Workcenter and for good deals, opt for easyInternetCafé (until 2am). 🕲 *Workcenter: C/ Roger de Lluria 2; Diagonal 439* 🕲 *easyInternetCafé: La Rambla 32; Ronda Universitat 35* 🕲 *People @ Web: C/Provença 367* • *93 207 01 97*

9 Courier Services

Courier services will pick up a package and deliver it anywhere in the world, usually within 1–5 days. 🕲 *Federal Express: 902 10 08 71* 🕲 *UPS: 902 88 88 20* 🕲 *DHL Worldwide Express: 902 12 24 24*

10 Fax

You can send and receive faxes at most post offices. Many internet centres also offer fax services, at considerably lower prices.

Streetsmart

Left **Guardia Urbana** Centre **Pharmacy shop front** Right **Pharmacy sign**

Security & Health Tips

Emergencies
The national emergency number is 112, through which you can contact the *policia* (police), *bombers* (firemen) and *ambulància* (ambulance).

Police
Dial 091 to call the national police (Policía Nacional), and 092 for the local police (Guàrdia Urbana). The Turisme Atenció centre, run by the Guàrdia Urbana and Turisme de Barcelona, provides advice and help to visitors who have been victims of crime. Ⓢ *Turisme Atenció • La Rambla 43 • 93 344 13 00 • Open 24 hours*

Personal Security
Although petty crime is rife, more serious incidences of violence are rare. Thieves occasionally carry knives – if threatened, hand over your belongings immediately.

Valuables
Leave all your valuables, including your passport, behind in a hotel safety deposit box. Take as little cash as possible and carry what you do have in a money belt hidden under clothes. Carry wallets in front pockets and ensure bags are strapped across your front. On the beach and in cafés and restaurants, always keep your belongings on your lap or tied to your person. Also be cautious of any odd or

unnecessary human contact, verbal or physical, whether it's a tap on the shoulder or someone spilling their drink at your table. Thieves often work in twos, so while one is catching your attention, the other is swiping your wallet.

Hospitals
Hospital de la Creu Roja de Barcelona, Hospital de la Santa Creu i de Sant Pau *(see p103)* and Hospital Clínic all have 24-hour emergency rooms (called *urgències*). For an ambulance, dial 061. Ⓢ *Hospital de la Creu Roja de Barcelona: C/Dos de Maig 301 • 93 433 15 51* Ⓢ *Hospital de la Santa Creu i de Sant Pau: C/Sant Antoni Maria Claret 167 • 93 291 90 00* Ⓢ *Hospital Clínic: C/Villaroel 170 • 93 227 54 00*

Doctors & Clinics
The tourist office can provide information on English-speaking doctors. There are numerous walk-in clinics in the city, including the Creu Blanca near Plaça de Catalunya, where there is no need to make an appointment. Ⓢ *Creu Blanca: C/Pelai 40 • 93 412 12 12 • Open 9am–1pm & 4–7pm Mon–Fri, 9am–1pm Sat*

Health Insurance
EU citizens can receive free medical care with a European health insurance card, which must be obtained

before travelling. Non-EU citizens are strongly advised to take out medical cover.

Dental Treatment
Dental care is not covered by the EU health service. There are numerous dental clinics in Barcelona where you can walk in and get a consultation, including the Clínica Dental Barcelona, where dentists are generally on duty 9am–midnight daily. Ⓢ *Clínica Dental Barcelona: Pg de Gràcia 97 • 93 487 83 29*

Pharmacies
Pharmacies *(farmàcies)* are marked by a large green cross, usually in neon. All chemists have trained pharmacists who can offer advice (places on and around La Rambla usually have a pharmacist who speaks English). Regular hours are generally 10am–10pm. One pharmacy per neighbourhood is open all night from 9pm until 9am on a rotating basis, (information is listed on the front door of each pharmacy). A number of places, particularly on La Rambla, stay open 24 hours a day.

Drinking Water
Spain's tap water is perfectly safe to drink. Most visitors, however, generally prefer to drink bottled water.

Streetsmart

Left **Caixa de Catalunya logo** Right **Twenty-euro note**

Banking & Money Tips

1 The Euro
Since 1 January 2002, the official currency of Spain, and much of Europe, has been the Euro. For general information on the Euro check the European Union website.
⌂ europa.eu.int/euro

2 Banks
Banks are generally open 8am–2pm on weekdays. Some are open 4–8pm on Thursdays and 8am–2pm on Saturdays, except from July to September. Banks tend to offer better exchange and commission rates than bureaux de change, although rates do vary from bank to bank. There's a Caixa de Catalunya exchange in Plaça de Catalunya, next to the tourist office, which stays open until 9pm. Numerous small bank branches exchange money in Estació de Sants train station and the airport; these are open from 7 or 8am to 10pm daily.

3 Changing Money
Avoid changing money at bureaux de change in tourist areas as commission rates tend to be high or exchange rates poor. On the whole, banks offer better deals, but bureaux de change have the advantage of longer opening hours. Some, particularly those on La Rambla, are open until midnight.

4 ATMs
ATMs (cash machines) provide the easiest way to access money and are a good way to beat commission charges. Surcharges depend on your bank. Relying on ATMs also means that you can take out money in smaller denominations and avoid carrying large amounts of cash. Before travelling, check with your bank that your PIN number works with foreign ATMs. Nearly all take VISA or MasterCard (Access) cards.

5 Traveller's Cheques
Buy traveller's cheques in Euros. All banks cash traveller's cheques, as do larger stores. Always carry the cheque numbers separately from the cheques. American Express traveller's cheques can be cashed free of charge at the American Express office and at any Banco Central Hispano; a passport is required.
⌂ American Express: La Rambla 74 • 91 393 82 16 • 9am–9pm Mon–Sat

6 Credit Cards
Visa and MasterCard are readily accepted in all but budget hotels, restaurants and shops. American Express can generally be used in hotels, but less often in restaurants and shops. Diner's Card is accepted in about 50 per cent of restaurants. Credit card cash advances are available from any bank (or ATM if you have a PIN number). Note that the transaction fee for cash advances on credit cards can be high.

7 Emergency Numbers
If your credit card is lost or stolen, call the police and your credit card company. Most credit cards have a number to call collect from abroad, which is provided at the time of issue. ⌂ Visa: 900 991 216 ⌂ MasterCard: 900 97 12 31 ⌂ American Express: 900 99 44 26

8 Online Banking
The quickest and cheapest way to keep track of your bank account and credit card bills is by checking them online. It's best to set up your online account before travelling.

9 Emergency Cash
It is advisable to carry some emergency cash hidden inside your luggage, separate from your wallet.

10 Tipping
Tipping is not the norm in Spain. In restaurants, most diners usually tip about five per cent of the bill. If you're eating a light meal, round up the bill to the nearest 50 cents. Taxi drivers are usually tipped five per cent and hotel porters about 50 cents per bag.

Left **Coffee and croissant** Right **Terrace café, Barri Gòtic**

10 Eating & Drinking Tips

1 Opening Hours
The Spanish eat much later than much of Europe; lunch starts around 2 or 3pm, with dinner any time after 9pm. Restaurants are usually open 1:30–4pm and 8:30–midnight. Many are closed one day of the week and during the month of August. Cafés and bars are open from around 7:30am, closing around 2am. It is difficult to get a drink or bite to eat after 4am.

2 The Menu
Multilingual menus are increasingly the norm. Many restaurants offer their best deal for lunch, so do as the Spaniards do and fill up from the *menú del dia* between 1:30 and 4pm. The fixed-price menu of the day usually includes three courses, wine and water.

3 Catalan Cuisine
Catalan cuisine is characterized by the meeting of *mar i muntanya* (surf and turf), and signature dishes include *llagosta i pollastre* (lobster and chicken). Side dish mainstays are *samfaina* (aubergine/eggplant, grilled peppers, tomatoes and onion in olive oil and garlic) and *escalivada* (sweet peppers, onion and garlic). Other Catalan favourites are *botifarra amb mongetes* (Catalan sausage with white beans) and *pa amb tomàquet* (bread smeared with tomato and

drizzled with olive oil). If innards are your thing, ask for *call* (tripe). For dessert, enjoy *crema catalana*, a custard topped with caramelized sugar.

4 Seafood & Paella
For prime seafood, head for the sea. Along Passeig Joan de Borbó in Barceloneta is a string of restaurants, many specializing in seafood and paellas. Seafood restaurants also abound in the Port Olímpic, where you can feast on fresh-off-the-boat fish and seafood on open-air terraces. Fresh seafood is served year-round, but the traditional day for paella is Thursday.

5 Vegetarian
Barcelona has a handful of vegetarian eateries. Carrer Pintor Fortuny, in El Raval, has a couple of options, including Biocenter (at number 25), with its all-you-can-eat salad bar. Vegetarians can also feast almost anywhere on an array of tapas, including *patates braves* (spicy potatoes) and *truita de patates* (potato omelette). If you eat fish, then you'll be spoiled for choice.

6 Seasonal Specialities
From the end of the year until mid-Spring, try the Catalan speciality of *calçots*, sweet grilled scallions usually in a *romesco* sauce (spicy tomato sauce). Another autumn favourite are *bolets* (mush-

rooms), usually lightly grilled and served with a sprinkling of olive oil.

7 Etiquette
Some restrictions for smoking in bars or restaurants apply from January 2006. Dress codes rarely apply.

8 Tipping
Tipping is not expected in most establishments, so it's up to your own preference and how you rate the service. If leaving a tip, five per cent is usually acceptable. In upscale restaurants, however, a tip of 10 per cent is the norm. Catalans occasionally tip at the bar, perhaps leaving the small change from their drinks bill.

9 Children
The Spanish are very relaxed about bringing children to restaurants and bars. Kids' menus are rare, though restaurants are often willing to serve half portions on request.

10 Disabled Access
All new restaurants must be wheelchair accessible by law, which includes access from the street to the dining room and at least one accessible bathroom. Contact the Institut Municipal de Persones amb Disminució *(see p134)* for a list of accessible restaurants. And always call ahead to double check.

For Barcelona's best restaurants & tapas bars **See pp44–5**

Left **Shopper, Pg de Gràcia** Centre **Shoe shop, C/Portaferrissa** Right **Clothes boutique, Gràcia**

🔟 Shopping Tips

Opening Hours
Most stores are open 10am to 2pm and 4:30pm to 8pm Monday to Saturday. Department stores and other large shops don't close at lunch time.

Sales
Barcelona's big sales (rebaixes) come twice a year, from 1 July to the end of August and from 7 January until the end of February.

Reclaiming VAT
Non-EU citizens can claim an IVA (VAT) refund on most purchases over €90 when they leave Spain. Shops displaying the tax-free logo will provide a tax-refundable receipt, which you present before checking-in on departure. IVA (VAT) of 16 per cent (7 per cent on food) is included in the advertised price. IVA for hotels is 7 per cent, which is not always included in the price.

Leather
Leather items are a good buy in Spain and are of high quality. There are good shoe stores on Carrer Portal de l'Àngel, Carrer Pelai, Rambla de Catalunya and Passeig de Gràcia. Loewe and Kastoria sell quality leather goods. ◎ Loewe: Pg de Gràcia 35 ◎ Kastoria: Av de la Catedral 6–8

Antiques
Antiques aficionados will be richly rewarded with a stroll along Carrer Banys Nous and Carrer de la Palla in the Barri Gòtic. For more antique finds, head to the Bulevard dels Antiquaris (see p50) on Passeig de Gràcia, home to over 60 antiques and arts shops. The antique markets, including the Mercat dels Antiquaris (see p53) and the Port Vell antique market, at weekends (10am–8pm), are also worth a browse.

Clothing
High-end clothing stores dot Passeig de Gràcia and Avinguda Diagonal. For trendier gear, head to Carrer Portaferrissa and Carrer Pelai. Spain's success story is the wildly popular men's and women's contemporary clothing chain Zara, which is all over town (and all over Europe). Another universal favourite is Mango, targeted towards younger women, which also has branches all over the city. If you're looking to buy local, there are a number of top-end Catalan designers, including Antonio Miró. ◎ Zara: Pg de Gràcia 16 ◎ Mango: Pg de Gràcia 65 ◎ Antonio Miró: C/Consell de Cent 349

Sizes
Clothing sizes tend to be small in Spain. Size conversions for women's clothing are: US/UK 6/8 is 36; 8/10 is 38; 10/12 is 40; 12/14 is 42; 14/16 is 44. For men's clothing, the conversions are: US & UK 36 is 46; 38 is 48; 40 is 50; 42 is 52.

Music
FNAC has a vast music selection, as does the department store El Corte Inglés. Equally popular among locals are the small eclectic music shops along Carrer Tallers (see p82). Also worth a look are the CD and vinyl music shops on nearby Carrer Riera Baixa (see p82). ◎ FNAC: El Triangle, Pl de Catalunya 4 ◎ El Corte Inglés: Portal de l'Àngel 19–21

Late-night Shops
Vip's is an all-purpose drugstore-bookstore-café, where you can buy books, gifts, beer, wine and snacks. Open Cor sells everything from fresh flowers to wrapping paper, beer and wine. ◎ Vip's: Rambla de Catalunya 7–9 • Open until 3am daily ◎ Open Cor: Ronda de Sant Pere 33 • Open until 2am daily

Department Stores
Barcelona's leading department store is El Corte Inglés, which has branches across the city. You can find seemingly everything under one roof, including a supermarket and a gourmet food shop. ◎ El Corte IngléWs: several locations, including Pl de Catalunya 14, Av Diagonal 471–473 & Av Diagonal 617–619

For Barcelona's best shopping areas **See pp50–51**

Left **Shop sale sign** Centre **Five-euro note** Right **Menú del Dia**

🔟 Barcelona on a Budget

1 Sightseeing Passes

The Barcelona Card offers up to 50 per cent off the city's main attractions, plus free travel on buses and the metro. It's available for two to five days at all tourist offices and El Corte Inglés department stores. The Articket, valid for three months, provides free entry to seven art museums, including MNAC *(see pp18–19)*, MACBA *(see pp28–9)* and the Fundació Joan Miró *(see pp22–3)*. The tourist office on Plaça de Catalunya *(see p134)* sells it, as do Caixa de Catalunya banks and the museums themselves.

2 Museums

Many museums offer free entry on the first Sunday of the month, including the Museu Picasso *(see pp24–5)* and MNAC *(see pp18–19)*. The tourist office has a list of all the free museum days. Most museums also offer a 30–50 per cent discount – or free admission – for people over 65.

3 Public Transport

The T-10 ticket permits 10 rides on metro, FGC and buses, but only lasts for 1 hour 15 minutes. Alternatively, you can purchase a two-, three-, four- or five-day pass, which provides unlimited travel on the same services. *See p131.*

4 Concerts & Opera

Enjoy rock-bottom prices for concerts and the opera (Sep–Jul) by buying seats with partial views – or no view at all. The Gran Teatre del Liceu *(see p66)* sells cheap tickets for opera and classical recitals. The Palau de la Música Catalana *(see pp26–7)* has reduced price early-evening weekend shows twice a month. For general information on cultural events – or visit the Institut de Cultura in the Palau de la Virreina *(see p13)*. 🕲 *Gran Teatre del Liceu ticket office: 93 485 99 00 Institut de Cultura: 93 301 77 75*

5 Eating

The most economical way to get a bite to eat is to pick up picnic goodies at one of the city's food markets *(see pp52–3)*. The *menú del dia* (fixed lunch menu) offered at many restaurants is another good way to fill up on the cheap. Dining on the terrace is often more pricey than eating inside, where sitting at the bar is usually the cheapest option.

6 Fast Food

Bypass McDonald's and Burger King and sample Spain's cheaper fast food equivalents. Pans & Company and Bocatta are found all over town; both offer cheap meals, particularly if you eat between 10am and noon, and 4 and 7pm.

7 Drinking

Start out the night in your hotel with a bottle of Spanish wine from the supermarket. Then head to the Barri Gòtic or El Raval where there are plenty of cheap dive bars. Order a *canya* (tap beer) or a Spanish bottled beer, Estrella or San Miguel, which are usually cheaper than imported beers.

8 Hotels

Visit Barcelona during the low season, from October to April, and you'll find cheaper hotel deals (and air fares). Enquire about special deals when booking a room – many places don't volunteer information on reductions unless specifically asked.

9 Hotel Bars

You don't have to stay at the ritzy hotels to enjoy their luxurious environs. Most of the bars and cafés at the five-star hotels are open to the general public. Try the Hotel Arts *(see p143)*, near the Port Olímpic, where you can sip a cocktail to the rippling tunes of classical piano.

10 Cinemas

Go to the cinema *(see p67)* on *el dia del espectador* (often Monday or Wednesday) or for a matinée (usually before 2:30pm), when tickets are cheaper.

Left **Overpriced eatery, La Rambla** Right **Traffic jam**

TOP10 Things to Avoid

Dangerous Areas

Beware of under-populated alleys and streets in the old town after dark, particularly in the Barri Gòtic and El Raval. These attract thieves who tend to operate in groups. Prime pickpocketing times are between 9pm and midnight, when most locals are eating dinner and only visitors are out on the streets. The early hours (3–6am), after the bars and clubs close, are also popular with thieves.

Overpriced Leather Shops

Avoid the pricey leather shops clustered on and around La Rambla. The leather is often poor quality and prices are high. Stop off at the tourist office for a list of approved leather shops, or head for established stores (see pp50–51).

La Rambla Scams

Don't get sidetracked by the raucous "find the hidden ball" games on La Rambla. Usually played on makeshift tables, presided over by a skilled, nimble-fingered trickster, it appears at first glance to be a lively game of chance. In reality, it's a confidence trick. The lively folk who cheer you on are all accomplices who are in on the act. Though you may win the first few rounds, you'll soon start to lose, and you'll walk away with a much lighter wallet. Also to be avoided are the gypsies who try to sell you flowers and often pick your pocket at the same time!

Overpriced Eats

Rip-off, touristy terrace restaurants line La Rambla. Most of these paella and tapas eateries cater solely to tourists, charging sky-high prices for mediocre meals. The side streets off La Rambla offer better food at more reasonable prices.

Crowds

Miss the crowds and interminably long queues at the city's most popular sights by visiting first thing in the morning when the sights open or towards the end of the day, an hour or two before closing time. To avoid the hordes on the beaches in summer go on weekday afternoons.

Money Exchange

Steer clear of the bureaux de change on La Rambla, Plaça de Cata-lunya and near major tourist sights. They usually charge much higher commission than banks. If they advertise no commission, exchange rates are generally poor.

Looking Like a Tourist

Avoid attracting attention to yourself as a tourist. Keep cameras hidden, try not to display large banknotes and don't wear valuable jewellery. When consulting a guidebook or map, keep a vigilant eye on your belongings.

Traffic

Avoid city traffic con-gestion by driving around late morning (10am–1pm) or late afternoon (5–7pm). Most office workers have a lunch break between 2pm and 4pm, which means that the roads are packed during this period. Similarly, avoid leaving town on Friday evenings, particularly during the summer. The best time to head out of the city is mid- to late-morning after 10am.

August

During the month of August, many Barcelona establishments shut down altogether, the locals disappear on holiday and the city fills with visitors. With so many restaurants, bars, shops and even some sights closed, not to mention the distinct lack of local life, August in Barcelona has its draw-backs. Always call first to check on opening times during this period.

Monday Sightseeing

Many of the top museums are closed on Mondays, including the Museu Picasso (see pp24–5) and the MNAC (see pp18–19). So always double-check opening times on this day.

Left **Room, Hotel Mesón Castilla** Right **Suite, Hotel Claris**

TOP 10 Accommodation Tips

Book Ahead
If visiting Barcelona in the high season (Mar–Sep), book ahead as the city's hotels, *pensions* and *hostals* (smaller, more basic guesthouses rated at one to three stars) usually fill to capacity. When reserving a room, ask about special deals as many hotels have these, especially in the low season (Oct–Mar).

Where to Find Budget Beds
There are scores of cheap *pensions* and *hostals* on La Rambla and its sidestreets in the Barri Gòtic and El Raval. Plaça Reial also has a cluster of budget accommodation options.

Pensions & Hostals
Room size (and comfort level) in *pensions* and *hostals* varies widely, but in the accredited budget places (the tourist office has a list of these), you'll find clean rooms and good security. Rooms come either *amb bany* (with a bath) or *sense bany* (without a bath); most have a washbasin.

Getting the Room you Want
Hotels and *hostals* give the best rooms to those who ask for them – so always inquire. Most *hostals*, particularly in the old town, have some rooms with lovely wrought-iron balconies,

which can make all the difference to a small room. Ask for *una habitació exterior amb vistes* (a room with a view) or *amb balcó* (with balcony). If you're a light sleeper, opt for a *una habitació interior* (interior room).

Single Travellers
Single rooms at *hostals* and *pensions* are few and far between, but hotels are legally obliged to let double rooms to single occupants at a fixed price. All rates must be posted at reception or in the rooms.

Families
Many hotels offer discounts for children under 12 when they share their parents' room on a temporary bed.

Security
If you're going to be staying at youth hostels and campsites, carry a chain and padlock to tie your luggage to something sturdy. Always leave your valuables in a safe or locked box, which most places have.

Hotel Booking Service & Websites
The tourist office *(see p132)* in Plaça de Catalunya has a hotel booking service, which is useful if you arrive in high season without a reservation. It offers bookings in hotels of all categories, but most often in three-star hotels and above. A

deposit is payable on reservation. The tourist office also produces a list of the best *pensions* and *hostals* for budget travellers. On the web, try www.barcelonahotels.es and www.barcelona turisme.com.

Cases de Pagès
Discover rural Catalonia by staying at *Cases de Pagès* (country or farm houses), which offer B&B-style lodgings. They vary widely, from small, rural homes with a handful of rooms to luxurious, palace-sized farmhouses. The high-end *Cases de Pagès* are called *Gîtes*. Stop by the Turisme de Catalunya office *(see p132)* for a free list of the *Gîtes de Catalunya* and (to buy) the *Cases de Pagès* book, which has detailed listings and pictures of all such houses. This information is also accessible through its website (www.gencat.es/probert).

Refugis
Throughout the Pyrenees and other mountainous areas, you'll find *refugis* (basic mountain hostels for hikers and bikers). They offer simple, cheap accommodation, usually bunk beds in a dorm room. In the summer months, *refugis* fill up quickly, so book in advance. Ask at tourist offices for a list of local ones; or stop by Turisme de Catalunya *(see p132)*.

Visitors seeking long-term accommodation, beware of agencies that charge for accommodation lists; they are invariably a scam.

Price Categories

For a standard, double room per night (with breakfast if included), taxes and extra charges.

€	Under €60
€€	€60–120
€€€	€120–180
€€€€	€180–240
€€€€€	Over €240

Exterior, Hotel Claris

🔟 Luxury Hotels

Hotel Arts
Barcelona's grande dame five-star hotel is mere steps from the sea, with ample, sumptuous rooms and top-notch eating places. The first-floor, outdoor pool has stunning views. Ⓢ *C/Marina 19–21* • *Map G5* • *93 221 10 00* • *www.hotelartsbarcelona. com* • *DA* • *€€€€€*

Hotel Claris
This exquisite, 19th-century Eixample palace was once home to the counts of Vedruna. Inside, you'll find a small museum of pre-Colombian art, part of the owner's collection, some of which also decorates the suites. Guests get free admission to the nearby Museu Egipci *(see p105)*, run by the hotel owner. Ⓢ *C/Pau Claris 150* • *Map E2* • *93 487 62 62* • *www.derby hotels.es* • *DA* • *€€€€€*

Hotel Palace Barcelona
This deluxe hotel, founded in 1919, is an emblem of tradition and style, with impeccable service. The acclaimed Restaurant Caelis, located in the old reading room, offers an innovative gourmet menu of New Spanish Cuisine. Ⓢ *Gran Vía de les Corts Catalanes, 668* • *Map F3* • *93 510 11 30* • *www. hotelpalacebarcelona.com* • *DA* • *€€€€€*

Hotel Majestic
Stately decor and faultless service are the hallmarks of this aptly named hotel. Exit through the heavy brass-and-glass doors and you're mere steps from the Eixample's *Modernista* gems. The rooftop swimming pool has views of the Sagrada Família and the Barcelona cityscape. Ⓢ *Pg de Gràcia 68* • *Map E2* • *93 488 17 17* • *www.hotelmajestic.es* • *DA* • *€€€€€*

Condes de Barcelona
The highlight of this magnificent *Modernista* hotel is its pentagonal lobby. The commodious rooms have classic, decor. Splash in the outdoor pool and dine at the Michelin-starred Lasarte restaurant. Ⓢ *Pg de Gràcia 73–75* • *Map E2* • *93 445 00 00* • *www.condesdebarcelona. com* • *DA* • *€€€€€*

Gallery Hotel
In the heart of the Eixample, this stylish hotel displays art and jewellery from local galleries in its lobby. The hotel café and restaurant have a lovely outdoor terrace, with live music in summer (Thu only). Ⓢ *C/ Rosselló 249* • *Map E2* • *93 415 99 11* • *www.gallery hotel.com* • *DA* • *€€€€€*

Princesa Sofia
Looming over uptown Barcelona, this luxury highrise hotel has a whopping 500 ample, dark-wood rooms, a fine restaurant and bar, and a half-indoor, half-outdoor pool. Popular for conferences, it has many meeting rooms and a business centre. Ⓢ *Pl Pio XII* • *Off map* • *93 508 10 00* • *www. princesasofia.com* • *DA* • *€€€€€*

Casa Camper
Dating from the 19th century, this hotel oozes with innovative yet comfortable design touches. Big rooms, roof-terrace, extraordinary vertical garden and a free 24-hour bar. Ⓢ *Elisabets 11* • *Map L2* • *93 342 62 80* • *www.casacamper.com* • *DA* • *€€€€€*

Hotel Rey Juan Carlos I
This massive complex includes a vast private garden and a conference hall for up to 2,500 people. The spacious rooms are sumptuously decorated in a contemporary style. The top floors offer unobstructed views of the city and mountains. Ⓢ *Av Diagonal 661–671* • *Off map* • *93 364 40 40* • *www.hrjuan carlos.com* • *DA* • *€€€€€*

1898
This colonial-style hotel recently opened in the former headquarters of a tobacco company dating from 1898. Its appeal is down to beautiful decor and soundproofed rooms equipped with the latest technology. Ⓢ *La Rambla 109* • *Map L2* • *93 552 95 52* • *www.barcelonahotel 1898.com* • *DA* • *€€€€€*

Left **Salon, Hotel Mesón Castilla** Right **Swimming Pool, Hotel Ducs de Bergara**

⑩ Historical Hotels

Hotel Mesón Castilla

A historical gem in the heart of El Raval, this family-run hotel is housed in an early-1900s mansion. A home-turned-hotel, it shines under the loving care of its management. From the opulent first-floor salon to the lovely rooms – each with antique furniture – this hotel offers a chance to step back in time. Enjoy breakfast on the outdoor patio. ⊗ *C/Valldonzella 5 • Map L1 • 93 318 21 82 • www. mesoncastilla.com • €€€*

Hotel Ducs de Bergara

Housed in a lovely 1898 *Modernista* building, this luxurious hotel has well-appointed rooms. There's a large interior courtyard with a swimming pool. ⊗ *C/Bergara 11 • Map L1 • 93 301 51 51 • www.hoteles-catalonia.es • DA • €€€€*

Avenida Palace

This is a classic hotel with contemporary rooms. The lobby showcases a lavish staircase with Baroque banisters. It was once a 19th-century tea parlour. ⊗ *Gran Via de les Corts Catalanes 605 • Map E3 • 93 301 96 00 • www.avenidapalace.com • DA • €€€€*

Hotel Neri

This 17th century former palace at the heart of the Barri Gòtic opened in 2003 and offers an exclusive combination of history, the avant-garde and glamour. There is internet access in all rooms, a library, solarium and a roof terrace with views to the Cathedral. ⊗ *C/Sant Sever 5 • Map M3 • 93 304 06 55 • www.hotelneri.com • €€€€*

Hotel Oriente

Opened in 1842, this Barri Gòtic institution has hosted its share of luminaries, including many opera greats from the nearby Liceu *(see p12)*. It was built on the site of an old Franciscan monastery and the ballroom was created out of the cloister. The hotel may be showing its age, but for many, its charm lies in the faded grandeur. ⊗ *La Rambla 45 • Map L4 • 93 302 25 58 • www.hotelhusaoriente. com • €€€*

Hotel Gran Via

Set in an elegant 1873 mansion, this hotel has maintained its historical allure, with suitably old-fashioned decor in the lobby and first-floor sitting room. Some rooms have been modernized, while others have antique furniture. One room is in a converted chapel, with Gothic ceilings. ⊗ *Gran Via de les Corts Catalanes 642 • Map E3 • 93 318 19 00 • www.nnhotels.es • DA • €€€*

Hotel Duquesa de Cardona

Located in a 16th-century building, this recently opened hotel combines the original structure with avant-garde decor and all the modern facilities. Most rooms have views of Montjuïc Mountain and the Olympic Port. ⊗ *Paseo Colón 12 • Map M6 • 93 268 90 90 • www.hduquesade cardona.com • €€€€€*

Hotel Montecarlo

This friendly, family-owned hotel, with a 1930s façade, is particularly eye-catching lit up at night. Rooms are pleasant and bright, and many have balconies overlooking La Rambla. ⊗ *La Rambla 124 • Map L2 • 93 412 04 04 • www.montecarlobcn. com • €€€€*

Nouvel

Just off La Rambla is this refurbished 1911 *Modernista* hotel. The modernized rooms are done up in cool tones with floral bedspreads. ⊗ *C/Santa Ana 18 • Map M2 • 93 301 82 74 • www. hotelnouvel.com • €€€*

Hotel España

Designed by architect Domènech i Montaner in 1899, this hotel is awash with Art Nouveau, including a restaurant rich with floral mosaics *(see p87)*. The rooms, in contrast to the ground-floor splendour, are all modern, if a little frayed around the edges. ⊗ *C/Sant Pau 9–11 • Map L4 • 93 318 17 58 • www.hotel espanya.com • DA • €€*

It is always worth checking hotel websites for off-season promotional offers.

Exterior, Hotel Colón

Price Categories

For a standard, double room per night (with breakfast if included), taxes and extra charges.

€ under €60
€€ €60–120
€€€ €120–180
€€€€ €180–240
€€€€€ over €240

TOP 10 Central Stays

Hotel Colón
A handsome, family-owned Barri Gòtic hotel, the Colón has traditional decor with mirrors and oil paintings throughout. The views of the Cathedral and Plaça de la Seu from this homely, quaint place, are stunning. ✆ Av de la Catedral 7 • Map N3 • 93 301 14 04 • www. hotelcolon.es •€€€€

Rivoli Ramblas
Contemporary elegance is the name of the game at this modern hotel. Look up to the hand-painted, domed ceiling in the lobby and down to the gleaming marble floors in the halls. Ample rooms are decorated in blonde wood and soft shades of purple and grey. Ask for a room with a balcony facing La Rambla for a front-row view of some of the city's best street theatre. ✆ La Rambla 128 • Map L2 • 934 81 76 76 • www.rivoli hotels.com • DA • €€€€€

Hotel Le Meridien
Rising gracefully over a bustling corner of La Rambla, the elegant and recently renovated Meridien offers lofty views of this famous street, the old town and the port. The rooms are decorated in warm shades. Live music is showcased in the bar Tue–Sat. ✆ La Rambla 111 • Map L2 • 93 318 62 00 • www.meridien barcelona.com • DA • €€€€

Hotel Banys Orientals
Behind the traditional frontage lies a modern, cosy hotel with free internet access in every room. The Cathedral, Picasso museum and Barceloneta beach are all close by. ✆ C/Argenteria 37 • Map N4 • 93 268 84 60 • www. hotelbanysorientals.com • €€

Barcelona Plaza Hotel
The large Plaza caters to the business traveller, with cosy rooms and a host of conference halls. The suite del rellotge (clock suite), located behind the façade's clock, is one of the most popular rooms, albeit the most pricey. ✆ Pl d'Espanya 6–8 • Map B3 • 93 426 26 00 • www.hoteles-catalonia.es • DA • €€€€

Rialto
Joan Miró fans will get a kick out of staying at the pleasant Rialto, housed in the building in which he was born. Miró prints adorn the rooms, which have hardwood floors and pale yellow furnishings. The hotel restaurant is decorated with splendid fossils, part of the owner's collection. ✆ C/Ferran 42 • Map M4 • 93 318 52 12 • www. hotel-rialto.com • DA • €€

Gran Hotel Barcino
This well-maintained hotel has a bright lobby with large windows – perfect for people-watching. Rooms are tastefully decorated in soft shades of grey and light-toned wood; the top rooms have partial views of the old town. ✆ C/Jaume I 6 • Map N4 • 93 302 20 12 • www.hotelbarcino.com • DA • €€€

Hotel Suizo
This hotel is just minutes from the major Barri Gòtic sights. Ask for a room with a balcony to enjoy lofty vistas of the plaça activity. ✆ Pl de l'Àngel 12 • Map N4 • 93 310 61 08 • www.hotel suizo.com • DA • €€€

Hotel Internacional
Most of the simple rooms at this popular place have wrought-iron balconies, ideal for taking in the all-day entertainment on La Rambla below. A continental buffet breakfast – served in a light, airy dining room – is included. ✆ La Rambla 78–80 • Map L4 • 93 302 25 66 • www.hotelhusa internacional.com • €€

Hotel Duc de la Victòria
Housed in a renovated mid-19th-century building, this modern hotel has bright rooms with tan-and-blue decor and dark wooden floors. Upper rooms offer views of the Cathedral and the Barri Gòtic. ✆ Duc de la Victòria 15 • Map M2 • 93 270 34 10 • www.hotelnhducdela victoria.com • DA • €€€

Unless otherwise stated, all hotels accept credit cards, have en-suite bathrooms & air conditioning.

Left **Hostal Jardi** Right **Entrance hall, Hostal Oliva**

Budget Accommodation

Hostal Residència Rembrandt
Spic-and-span rooms, some with en-suite bathrooms, and a friendly, international staff, make for a great, all-round *hostal*. Ask for an exterior room, most of which have wrought-iron balconies that are perfect for checking out the Barri Gòtic action below. ✪ C/Portaferrissa 23 • Map M3 • 93 318 10 11 • www.hostalrembrandt.com • €

Hostal Oliva
From the lovely, *Modernista* elevator to the individually wrapped soaps imprinted with the Oliva logo, this cheerful, family-run *hostal* is one of Barcelona's best. The ornate *Modernista* building has bright rooms that are sparklingly clean; some have en-suite bathrooms. ✪ Pg de Gràcia 32 • Map E3 • 93 488 01 62 • www.lasguias.com/hostaloliva • No credit cards • €€

Hostal Goya
A well-run *hostal* that has been accommodating visitors since 1952. The newly renovated first floor has airy rooms in tan and blonde wood. The charming older floor upstairs is less expensive, with original tiled floors from the late 1800s. Most rooms have en-suite bathrooms and some have air-conditioning. ✪ C/Pau Claris 74 • Map N1 • 93 302 25 65 • www.hostalgoya.com • €€

Hostal Fernando
Spotless and bright, this central *hostal* has well-maintained doubles (with or without bath), plus dorm rooms that sleep 4 to 8 people. There are also left-luggage lockers. ✪ C/Ferran 31 • Map L4 • 93 343 79 93 • www.barcelona-on-line.es/fernando • €

Hostal Ciudad Condal
This friendly, family-owned *hostal* is housed in an elegant *Modernista* building. Simple but well-kept rooms vary in size; if you'd like city views, ask for a balconied room overlooking Carrer Mallorca. For some quiet, opt for a room facing the interior courtyard and garden. ✪ C/Mallorca 255 • Map E2 • 93 215 10 40 • €€

Hostal Jardí
Get your beauty sleep in the snug heart of the Barri Gòtic at this hotel. Newly renovated rooms, all with en-suite bathrooms, are done up in light wood and cool colours. The bright breakfast room has balconies overlooking the plaça. ✪ Pl Sant Josep Oriol 1 • Map M3 • 93 301 59 00 • €€

Hostal Parisien
The well-maintained Parisien, with its clean rooms (some with en-suite bathrooms) and a TV lounge, is run by an amiable English-speaking couple. Some rooms overlook La Rambla, while others face a backstreet – less entertaining, but also less noisy. ✪ La Rambla 114 • Map L4 • 93 301 62 83 • No credit cards • €

Hostal Opera
Don't expect luxury, but rooms are clean, comfortable and all have bathrooms – and the *hostal* has a great location round the corner from La Rambla. ✪ Sant Pau 20 • Map L4 • 93 318 82 01 • www.hostalopera.com • €

Hostal Eden
A tidy, well-run *hostal*, which is housed on several floors of an up-market apartment building. The newer rooms all have large bathrooms and air-conditioning; some are also equipped with a small refrigerator. Guests have access to a coin-operated, web-connected computer. ✪ C/Balmes 55 • Map E2 • 93 452 66 20 • www.hostaleden.net • €€

Hostal Béjar
If you're arriving late at the Sants railway station, this *hostal*, just a ten-minute walk away, is a good bet. Call ahead in high season. Rooms are basic and clean, and all doubles have en-suite bathrooms. There's a sitting room with TV and you also have use of a refrigerator. ✪ C/Béjar 36–38 • Map B2 • 93 325 59 53 • www.hostalbejar.com • €

Unless otherwise stated, none of these establishments has air-conditioning or en-suite bathrooms.

Price Categories

For a standard, double room per night (with breakfast if included), taxes and extra charges.	€	under €60
	€€	€60–120
	€€€	€120–180
	€€€€	€180–240
	€€€€€	over €240

First floor, Gothic Point Youth Hostel

🔟 Hostels & Student Residences

Streetsmart

1 Gothic Point Youth Hostel

This bright, well-run, central hostel has dorm rooms sleeping 8 to 16. Breakfast is included in the price, and there's free 24-hour internet access. There is air-conditioning in all rooms. ✪ C/Vigatans 5 • Map N4 • 93 268 78 08 • www.gothicpoint.com • €

2 Ideal Youth Hostel

Situated close to La Rambla, this is a modern hostel with dorms for 4, 6 and 8 people, each with balcony, en-suite toilet and shower. Breakfast is included as is free internet access. There is a self-service laundrette. ✪ C/Unió 12 • Map L4 • 93 342 61 77 • www.idealhostel.com • €

3 Alberg Mare de Déu de Montserrat

This large hostel is quite a distance from the city centre, but it's within walking distance of the Vallcarca metro stop. A continental breakfast is included in the price, and the services on offer include laundry, a TV room, coin-operated internet access and a cheap cafeteria. Dorms sleep 6 to 12. ✪ Pg de la Mare de Déu del Coll 41–51 • Off map • 93 210 51 51 • www.tujuca.com • DA • €

4 Alberg Juvenil Palau

Small yet wonderfully central, this hostel has basic dorm rooms for 4 to 8. Breakfast is included, and guests have the use of a kitchen. ✪ C/del Palau 6 • Map M4 • 93 412 50 80 • 3am curfew • www.bcnalberg.com • €

5 Alberg Kabul

Kabul is a favourite with young backpackers, so it's often full (and noisy). Dorm rooms, all with air-conditioning and some with balconies on the Plaça Reial (see p36), sleep 4 to 20 people. There's a laundry, free internet access, lockers and a small cafeteria that serves cheap food during the day. ✪ Pl Reial 17 • L4 • 93 318 51 90 • www.kabul.es • €

6 Alberg Pere Tarrès

This friendly hostel is some distance from the city centre, but within walking distance of Maria Cristina and Les Corts metro stops. The dorms sleep 2 to 8; all have bathrooms and air-conditioning. There are laundry facilities, plus coin-operated internet access and the use of a kitchen and two terraces. ✪ C/Numància 149 • Off map • 93 410 23 09 • www.peretarres.org/alberg • DA • €

7 Centric Point Hostel

Housed in a renovated Modernista building, this hostel offers large dorms, as well as single and double rooms with private facilities. There is also a common room with a bar, free internet access and satellite TV. ✪ Passeig de Gràcia 33 • Map E3 • 93 231 20 45 • www. centricpointhostel.com • €

8 Alberg Can Soleret

This hostel in the coastal town of Mataró, 30 km (19 miles) north of Barcelona, is easily accessible by train. Its rooms, in a 19th-century country house, have 4 to 16 beds, most with views of the sea. There's a TV lounge and a terrace with ping-pong. Hiking and biking excursions can be organized. ✪ Torrent de les Piques 52, Mataró • Off map • 93 757 57 07 • Midnight curfew • No credit cards • Reservations essential • DA • €

9 Alberg La Ciutat

In the neighbourhood of Gràcia, this hostal residència, popular with students, has simple, well-kept double and single rooms, with washbasins and en-suite toilets. ✪ C/l'Alegre de Dalt 66 • Off map • 93 213 03 00 • DA • Closed Oct–Jun • €

10 Sun and Moon Hostel

Close to all the major attractions in the old town, this recently renovated residence has clean rooms that sleep up to 8 people, with private bathrooms and air-conditioning. Free lockers are available, as is bike hire. ✪ Ferran 17 • Map M4 • 93 270 20 60 • www.smhostel.net • €

Unless otherwise stated, these hostels & student residences do not have air-conditioning or en-suite bathrooms.

147

Left **Camping Tamariu** Right **Swimming Pool, Aparthotel Bertran**

Campsites & Aparthotels

1 Camping Roca-Grosa

Situated between the mountains and the sea, this modern campsite has good installations and access to the nearby beach. It also has a large swimming pool, restaurant and bar and is 1 km away from the lively resort of Calella. Bungalows are also available. ⬉ *Ctra, N-II km 665, Calella • 93 769 12 97 • www.rocagrossa.com • €*

2 Camping Sitges

A small and well-kept campsite with swimming pool, supermarket and playground. It is located 2 km (1 mile) southward from Sitges, and is close to its famous beaches. ⬉ *Ctra, Comarcal 246, km 38, Sitges • 93 894 10 80 • www.campingsitges.com • Closed mid-Oct–Feb • €*

3 Camping Masnou

Located 12 km (7.5 miles) to the north of Barcelona, this family-owned camp site faces the sea and has a small beach nearby. Facilities include a supermarket, restaurant and bar. ⬉ *Camil Fabra 33 (N-II, km 663), El Masnou • 93 555 15 03 • Credit cards from €100 • DA • €*

4 Camping Tamariu

This well-kept camp site is on the Costa Brava, near the lovely beach town of Tamariu. It's 200 m (656 ft) from the beach and within sauntering distance of the town for bars, restaurants and grocery shops. ⬉ *Costa Rica 2, near Tamariu, 5 km E of Palafrugell • 972 62 04 22 • www.campingtamariu. com • Closed Oct–Apr • €*

5 Camping Playa Sol

Twenty-eight km (17.5 miles) north of Barcelona is this campsite next to a small beach. It is also close to several larger beaches. The camp site is about 1 km (0.6 mile) from the train station. Bungalows are also available. ⬉ *Carretera A2, km 650, 8 km E of Mataró • 93 790 47 20 • www.campingplayasol.com • Closed Nov–Mar • DA • €*

6 Camping Globo Rojo

Close to the beaches of Canet de Mar and with a swimming pool, tennis court, football pitch as well as all kinds of sporting activities. Great for kids. ⬉ *Ctra, N-II km 660, 9, Canet de Mar • 93 794 11 43 • www.globo-rojo.com • Closed mid-Oct–Apr • DA • €*

7 Citadines

If you're smitten with Barcelona, try an aparthotel for a longer stay. The Citadines aparthotel on La Rambla has well-appointed studios and small apartments with amenities, such as a kitchen (with oven and microwave), iron and a CD stereo. The rooftop solarium, equipped with beach chairs and showers, is just the spot to unwind. ⬉ *La Rambla 122 • Map L2 • 93 270 11 11 • www. citadines.com • €€*

8 Aparthotel Bertran

This aparthotel has ample studios and apartments (many with balconies), a rooftop terrace with swimming pool, a small gym and 24-hour laundry service. Breakfast is served in your apartment. ⬉ *C/Bertran 150 • 93 212 75 50 • www.hotelbertran. com • €€€*

9 Atenea Aparthotel

Designed with business travellers in mind, this top-notch aparthotel sits near Barcelona's business and financial district around upper Diagonal. Rooms are ample and well-equipped, and there are several conference rooms and a 24-hour laundry service. ⬉ *C/ Joan Güell 207–211 • 93 490 66 40 • www.apart hotelatenea.com • €€€*

10 Habit Servei

This agency can help find furnished apartments for both short- and long-term stays. They can also find flat-shares for varying lengths of time. The average cost is around €700 a month ⬉ *C/ Muntaner 200 • Map D2 • 93 240 50 23 • www.habitservei.com*

 Unless otherwise stated, all campsites are open all year round, though many open only at weekends October–March.

Coastline, Costa Brava

Price Categories

For a standard, double room per night (with breakfast if included), taxes and extra charges.

€	under €60
€€	€60–120
€€€	€120–180
€€€€	€180–240
€€€€€	over €240

🔟 Getaways Beyond Barcelona

1 La Torre del Remei

Close to the Pyrenean town of Puigcerdà, this restored 1910 *Modernista* palace, with its series of sumptuous rooms, has an outdoor heated pool and a renowned restaurant. Take your pick of views: impressive mountain peaks or the lush garden. 🛇 *Camí Reial, Bolvir, 3 km SW of Puigcerdà • 972 14 01 82 • www.relais chateaux.com • €€€€€*

2 El Hostal de la Gavina

This elegant mansion, set in peaceful grounds, is just 200 m (656 ft) from the beach. The rooms have antique furniture and fixtures, and there's a saltwater pool. The first-rate restaurant serves divine Mediterranean fare. 🛇 *Pl de la Rosaleda, 3km S of S'Agaró • 972 32 11 00 • www.lagavina.com • Closed mid-Oct–Easter (except New Year) • €€€€€*

3 Hotel Aiguablava

This coastal institution is perched atop rugged cliffs overlooking the Mediterranean. It is run by the fourth generation of the same family. Many of the rooms – each individually decorated – have splendid vistas of the sea. There's a large outdoor pool and breakfast is included. 🛇 *Platja de Fornells, Begur • 972 62 45 62 • www. aiguablava.com • Closed Nov–Feb • €€€*

4 Fonda Biayna

The Fonda Biayna has been in operation since the 1820s. Wood-beamed ceilings and antique furniture imbue it with rustic flair. The inn's most famous guest was Picasso, who arrived here by mule en route to Paris (with paintings in tow). 🛇 *C/de Sant Roc 11, Bellver de Cerdanya • 973 51 04 75 • www. fondabiayna.com • €€*

5 Hostal Sa Tuna

Take in the sea views from your terrace at this five-room, family-run hotel on the pretty Platja Sa Tuna. The restaurant serves excellent Catalan cuisine and breakfast is included. 🛇 *Pg de Ancora 6, Platja Sa Tuna, 5 km N of Begur • 972 62 21 98 • www.hostalsatuna.com • Closed Oct–Mar • €€€*

6 Mas de Torrent

Get some old-fashioned comfort in a beautifully restored 18th-century farmhouse near Pals. Antique decor is offset by museum-worthy contemporary art. There's an outdoor pool. 🛇 *Finca Mas de Torrent, Torrent, 5 km NW of Palafrugell • 972 30 32 92 • www.relaischateaux. com • DA • €€€€€*

7 Parador de Tortosa

Looming over the town of Tortosa is the ancient Arab Castillo de la Zuda, within which this parador is housed. Decor is suitably old-world, with dark-wood furniture and antique fixtures, and the view of countryside and mountains is superb. 🛇 *Castillo de la Zuda, Tortosa • 977 44 44 50 • www.parador.es • €€€*

8 Ca L'Aliu

This restored, cosy *casa rural* is in the tiny medieval town of Peratallada. Comfortable rooms all have antique furniture. The amiable owners will lend you bikes. 🛇 *C/Roca 6, Peratallada, 12 km NW of Palafrugell • 972 63 40 61 • www.calaliu.com • €€*

9 Royal Tanau

This luxury hotel, has chair lifts direct to the slopes of the ski resort Baqueira-Beret *(see p120)*. Cosy cabin-style rooms offer sweeping views of the peaks. 🛇 *Ctra/de Beret, Baqueira-Beret, 12 km N of Lleida • 973 64 44 46 • www.meliaroyaltanau. solmelia.com • Closed May–Nov • DA • €€€€€*

10 El Paller de Can Viladomat

Visit the Catalonian interior from this rustic, 18th-century country home. Rooms are simple but comfortable, and breakfast and a home-cooked dinner are included in the price. There's also a small swimming pool. 🛇 *Can Viladomat, Navès, 19 km E of Solsona • 973 29 90 26 • www. agronet.org/elpaller • No credit cards • €*

General Index

Acknowledgements

The Authors

AnneLise Sorensen is a travel writer currently based in Barcelona. She has written and edited on numerous magazines and travel guides, covering destinations such as Spain, Denmark, California and Ireland.

Ryan Chandler is a writer and journalist who has been working in Barcelona for over ten years. He currently works as Barcelona correspondent for the Spanish magazine *The Broadsheet*.

Produced by Departure Lounge, London

Editorial Director Ella Milroy
Art Editor Lee Redmond
Editor Clare Tomlinson
Designer Lisa Kosky
DTP Designer Ingrid Vienings
Picture Researcher Monica Allende
Research Assistance Amaia Allende, Ana Virginia Aranha, Diveen Henry
Consultant Brian Catlos
Proofreader Catherine Day
Indexer Hilary Bird
Fact Checkers Paula Canal, Brian Catlos, AnneLise Sorensen

Photographers Joan Farré, Manuel Huguet

Additional photography Max Alexander, Mike Dunning, Heidi Grassley, Alan Keohane, Ella Milroy, Naomi Peck, Paul Young

Illustrators Chris Orr & Associates, Lee Redmond

Maps Martin Darlison, Tom Coulson, Encompass Graphics Ltd

AT DORLING KINDERSLEY
Senior Publishing Manager
Louise Bostock Lang
Publishing Manager Kate Poole
Senior Art Editor Marisa Renzullo
Art Director Gillian Allan
Publisher Douglas Amrine
Cartography Co-ordinator Casper Morris
DTP Jason Little, Conrad van Dyk
Production Joanna Bull

Design and Editorial Assistance
Caroline Mead, Pete Quinlan, Mani Ramaswamy, Sylvia Tombesi-Walton

Picture Credits

Placement Key: t-top;tc-top centre; tr-top right; cla-centre left above; ca-centre above; cra-centre right above; cl-centre left; c-centre; cr-centre right; clb-centre left below; cb-cent-re below; crb-centre right below; bl-below left; bc below centre; br below right.

Works of art have been reproduced with permission of the following copyright holders: *Homea* 1974 Eduardo Arranz Bravo © ADAGP, Paris and DACS, London 2006 28br; *Rainy Taxi* Salvador Dalí © Kingdom of Spain, Gala– Salvador Dalí Foundation, DACS, London 2006 119b.

The publishers would like to thank the following individuals, companies and picture libraries for permission to reproduce their photographs:

AISA, Barcelona: 1c, 11c, 30tl, 30tr, 30c, 31bl, 31tr, 31cr, 31br, 118c; BARCELONA TURISME: 61tr; 110c; Espai d'Imatge 64c; 65b; Jordi Trullas 64t; CASA ALFONSO: 108tr; DANIEL CAMPI: 146tl; EGO GALLERY: 84tl; GETTY IMAGES: Tony Stone/Luc Beziat 48c; MANUEL HUGUET: 128–9; IMAGESTATE: AGE-Fotostock 141tr; Courtesy of CAIXA CATALUNYA: 137tl; FUNDACION JOAN MIRO: *Pagès Català al cla de Luna* Joan Miró © Sucession Miró/ADAGP, Paris and DACS, London 2006 22bl; *Tapis de al Fundacio* Joan Miró © Sucession Miró/ADAGP, Paris and DACS, London 2006 22–3c; *Home i Dona Davant un Munt d'Excrement* Joan Miró © Sucession Miró/ADAGP, Paris and DACS, London 2006 23tr; JAMBOREE: 47tr; MUSEU NACIONAL d'ART DE CATALUNYA: 18b; 19tl; 19tr; 19ca; 19b; 92–93; MUSEU d'ART CONTEMPORANI: 28tl; 28cl; 28–29c; MUSEU PICASSO: *Hombre con Boina* Pablo Picasso © Sucession Picasso/DACS, London 2006 24b; *La Espera* Pablo Picasso © Sucession Picasso/DACS, London 2006 24–5; *El Loco* Pablo Picasso © Sucession Picasso/DACS, London 2006 25t; *Sketch for Guernica* Pablo Picasso © Sucession Picasso/DACS, London 2006 25cr; *Las Meninas* Pablo Picasso © Sucession Picasso/DACS, London 2006 25b; MIRIAM NEGRE: 44tr; 46bl; 58bl; 114l; 144r; 112b; 113t; 117; 139r; PARC ZOOLOGIC: 16bl; FRANCISCO FERNANDEZ PRIETO: 76tl; 76tr; PRISMA, Barcelona: 66b; 125t; 126t; RAZZMATAZZ: Albert Uriach 47cl; 100tr; SIDECAR FACTORY CLUB: Moises Torne (motobi@terra.es) 77tl.

All other images are © Dorling Kindersley. For further information see www.dkimages.com.

English-Catalan Phrase Book

In an Emergency

Help!	**Auxili!**	ow-**gzee**-lee
Stop!	**Pareu!**	**pah**-reh-oo
Call a doctor!	**Telefoneu un metge!**	teh-leh-fon-**eh**-oo oon **meh**-djuh
Call an ambulance!	**Telefoneu una ambulància!**	teh-leh-fon-**eh**-oo oo-nah ahm-boo-**lahn**-see-ah
Call the police!	**Telefoneu la policia**	teh-leh-fon-**eh**-oo lah poh-lee **see**-ah
Call the fire brigade!	**Telefoneu els bombers!**	teh-leh-fon-eh-oo uhlz boom-**behs**
Where is the nearest telephone?	**On és el telèfon més proper?**	on-ehs uhl tuh-leh fon mehs proo-**peh**
Where is the nearest hospital?	**On és l'hospital més proper?**	on-ehs looss-pee-tahl mehs proo-**peh**

Communication Essentials

Yes	**Sí**	see
No	**No**	noh
Please	**Si us plau**	sees **plah**-oo
Thank you	**Gràcies**	**grah**-see-uhs
Excuse me	**Perdoni**	puhr-**thoh**-nee
Hello	**Hola**	**oh**-lah
Goodbye	**Adéu**	ah-they-**oo**
Good night	**Bona nit**	**bo**-nah neet
Morning	**El matí**	uhl muh-**tee**
Afternoon	**La tarda**	lah **tahr**-thuh
Evening	**El vespre**	uhl **vehs**-pruh
Yesterday	**Ahir**	ah-**ee**
Today	**Avui**	uh-**voo**-ee
Tomorrow	**Demà**	duh-**mah**
Here	**Aquí**	uh-**kee**
There	**Allà**	uh-**lyah**
What?	**Què?**	keh
When?	**Quan?**	kwahn
Why?	**Per què?**	puhr keh
Where?	**On?**	ohn

Useful Phrases

How are you?	**Com està?**	kom uhs-**tah**
Very well, thank you.	**Molt bé, gràcies.**	mol **beh grah**-see-uhs
Pleased to meet you.	**Molt de gust.**	mol duh **goost**
See you soon.	**Fins aviat.**	feenz uhv-**yat**
That's fine.	**Està bé.**	uhs-**tah** beh
Where is/are ..?	**On és/són?**	ohn ehs/sohn
How far is it to..?	**Quants metres/ kilòmetres hi ha d'aquí a ...?**	kwahnz meh- truhs/kee-**loh**- muh-truhs yah dah-**kee** uh
Which way to ...?	**Per on es va a ...?**	puhr **on** uhs **bah** ah
Do you speak English?	**Parla anglès? ...**	**par**-luh an-**glehs**
I don't understand	**No l'entenc.**	noh luhn-**teng**

Could you speak more slowly, please?	**Pot parlar més a poc a poc, si us plau?**	pot par-**lah** mehs pok uh pok sees plah-oo
I'm sorry.	**Ho sento.**	oo **sehn**-too

Useful Words

big	**gran**	gran
small	**petit**	puh-**teet**
hot	**calent**	kah-**len**
cold	**fred**	fred
good	**bo**	boh
bad	**dolent**	doo-**len**
enough	**bastant**	bahs-**tan**
well	**bé**	beh
open	**obert**	oo-**behr**
closed	**tancat**	tan-**kat**
left	**esquerra**	uhs-**kehr**-ruh
right	**dreta**	**dreh**-tuh
straight on	**recte**	**rehk**-tuh
near	**a prop**	uh **prop**
far	**lluny**	**lyoon**-yuh
up/over	**a dalt**	uh **dahl**
down/under	**a baix**	uh **bah**-eeshh
early	**aviat**	uhv-**yat**
late	**tard**	tahrt
entrance	**entrada**	uhn-**trah**-thuh
exit	**sortida**	soor-**tee**-thuh
toilet	**lavabos/ serveis**	luh-**vah**-boos sehr-**beh**-ees
more	**més**	mess
less	**menys**	**men**-yees

Shopping

How much does this cost?	**Quant costa això?**	kwahn kost ehs-**shoh**
I would like ...	**M'agradaria ...**	muh-**grah-thuh- ree**-ah
Do you have?	**Tenen?**	**tehn**-un
I'm just looking, thank you	**Només estic mirant, gràcies.**	noo-mess ehs- teek mee-**rahn grah**-see-uhs
Do you take credit cards?	**Accepten targes de crèdit?**	ak-**sehp**-tuhn tahr-**zhuhs** duh **kreh**-deet
What time do you open?	**A quina hora obren?**	ah **keen**-uh **oh**-ruh **oh**-bruhn
What time do you close?	**A quina hora tanquen?**	ah **keen**-uh oh -ruh **tan**-kuhn
This one.	**Aquest**	ah-**ket**
That one.	**Aquell**	ah-**kehl**
expensive	**car**	kahr
cheap	**bé de preu/ barat**	beh thuh preh- oo/bah-**rat**
size (clothes)	**talla/mida**	**tah**-lyah/**mee**-thuh
size (shoes)	**número**	**noo**-mehr-oo
white	**blanc**	blang
black	**negre**	**neh**-gruh
red	**vermell**	vuhr-**mel**
yellow	**groc**	grok

green	verd	behrt
blue	blau	blah-oo
antique store	antiquari/	an-tee-kwah-ree/
	botiga	boo-**tee**-gah/dan-
	d'antiguitats	**tee**-ghee-**tats**
bakery	el forn	uhl **forn**
bank	el banc	uhl **bang**
book store	la llibreria	lah lyee-bruh-**ree**-ah
butcher's	la carnisseria	**lah kahr**-nee-suh-**ree**-ah
pastry shop	la pastisseria	lah pahs-tee-suh-**ree**-uh
chemist's	la farmàcia	lah fuhr-**mah**-see-ah
fishmonger's	la peixateria	lah peh-shuh-tuh-**ree**-uh
greengrocer's	la fruiteria	lah froo-**ee**-tuh-**ree**-uh
grocer's	la botiga de queviures	lah boo-**tee**-guh duh keh-vee-**oo**-ruhs
hairdresser's	la perruqueria	lah peh-roo-kuh-**ree**-uh
market	el mercat	uhl muhr-**kat**
newsagent's	el quiosc de premsa	uhl kee-**ohsk** duh **prem**-suh
post office	l'oficina de correus	loo-fee-**see**-nuh duh koo-**reh**-oos
shoe store	la sabateria	lah sah-bah-tuh-**ree**-uh
supermarket	el supermercat	uhl soo-puhr-muhr-**kat**
tobacconist's	l'estanc	luhs-**tang**
travel agency	l'agència de viatges	la-**jen**-see-uh duh vee-**ad**-juhs

Sightseeing

art gallery	la galeria d'art	lah gah-luh-**ree**-yuh **dart**
cathedral	la catedral	lah kuh-tuh-**thrahl**
church	l'església	luhz-**gleh**-zee-uh
	la basílica	lah buh-**zee**-lee-kuh
garden	el jardí	uhl zhahr-**dee**
library	la biblioteca	lah bee-blee-oo-**teh**-kuh
museum	el museu	uhl moo-**seh**-oo
tourist infor mation office	l'oficina de turisme	loo-fee-**see**-nuh thuh too-**reez**-muh
town hall	l'ajuntament	luh-djoon-tuh-**men**
closed for holiday	tancat per vacances	tan-**kat** puhr bah-**kan**-suhs
bus station	l'estació d'autobusos	luhs-tah-see-**oh** dow-toh-**boo**-zoos
railway station	l'estació de tren	luhs-tah-see-**oh** thuh **tren**

Staying in a Hotel

Do you have a vacant	¿Tenen una habitació	**teh**-nuhn **oo**-nuh ah-bee-tuh-see-**oh**
room?	lliure?	**lyuh**-ruh
double room with double bed	habitació doble amb llit de matrimoni	ah-bee-tuh-see-**oh** **doh**-bluh am **lyeet** duh mah-tree-**moh**-nee
twin room	habitació amb dos llits/ amb llits individual	ah-bee-tuh-see-**oh** am dohs **lyeets**/s am **lyeets** in-thee-vee-thoo-**ahls**
single room	habitació individual	ah-bee-tuh-see-**oh** een-dee-vee-thoo-**ahl**
room with a bath	habitació amb bany	ah-bee-tuh-see-**oh** am **bah**nyuh
shower	dutxa	**doo**-chuh
porter	el grum	uhl **groom**
key	la clau	lah **klah**-oo
I have a reservation	Tinc una habitació reservada	**ting** oo-nuh ah-bee-tuh-see-**oh** reh-sehr-**vah**-thah

Eating Out

Have you got a table for...	Tenen taula per...?	**teh**-nuhn **tow**-luh puhr
I would like to reserve a table.	Voldria reservar una taula.	vool-**dree**-uh reh-sehr-**vahr** **oo**-nuh **tow**-luh
The bill please	El compte, si us plau.	uhl **kohm**-tuh sees **plah**-oo
I am a vegetarian	Sóc vegetarià/ vegetariana	**sok** buh-zhuh-tuh-ree-**ah** buh-zhuh-tuh-ree-**ah**-nah
waitress	cambrera	kam-**breh**-ruh
waiter	cambrer	kam-**breh**
menu	la carta	lah **kahr**-tuh
fixed-price menu	menú del dia	muh-**noo** thuhl **dee**-uh
wine list	la carta de vins	ah **kahr**-tuh thuh **veens**
glass of water	un got d'aigua	oon **got** dah-ee-gwah
glass of wine	una copa de vi	oo-nuh **ko**-pah thuh **vee**
bottle	una ampolla	oo-nuh am-**pol**-yuh
knife	un ganivet	oon gun-ee-**veht**
fork	una forquilla	oo-nuh foor-**keel**-yuh
spoon	una cullera	oo-nuh kool-**yeh**-ruh
breakfast	l'esmorzar	les-moor-**sah**
lunch	el dinar	uhl dee-**nah**
dinner	el sopar	uhl soo-**pah**
main course	el primer plat	uhl pree-**meh** plat
starters	els entrants	uhlz ehn-**tranz**
dish of the day	el plat del dia	uhl **plat** duhl **dee**-uh
coffee	el cafè	uhl kah-**feh**
rare	poc fet	pok **fet**
medium	al punt	ahl **poon**
well done	molt fet	mol **fet**

Menu Decoder

l'aigua mineral	**lah**-ee-gwuh mee-nuh-**rahl**	mineral water
sense gas/	sen-zuh gas/	still
amb gas	am gas	sparkling
al forn	ahl **forn**	baked
l'all	**lahl**lyuh	garlic
l'arròs	lahr-**roz**	rice
les botifarres	lahs **boo**-tee-fah-rahs	sausages
la carn	lah **karn**	meat
la ceba	lah **seh**-buh	onion
la cervesa	lah-sehr-**ve**-sah	beer
l'embotit	lum-boo-**teet**	cold meat
el filet	uhl fee-**let**	sirloin
el formatge	uhl for-**mah**-djuh	cheese
fregit	freh-**zheet**	fried
la fruita	lah froo-**ee**-tah	fruit
els fruits secs	uhlz froo-**eets** seks	nuts
les gambes	lahs **gam**-bus	prawns
el gelat	uhl djuh-**lat**	ice cream
la llagosta	lah lyah-**gos**-tah	lobster
la llet	lah **lyet**	milk
la llimona	lah lyee-**moh**-nah	lemon
la llimonada	lah lyee-moh-**nah**-tuh	lemonade
la mantega	lah mahn-**teh**-gah	butter
el marisc	uhl muh-**reesk**	seafood
la menestra	lah muh-**nehs**-truh	vegetable stew
l'oli	**loll**-ee	oil
les olives	luhs oo-**lee**-vuhs	olives
l'ou	**loh**-oo	egg
el pa	uhl **pah**	bread
el pastís	uhl pahs-**tees**	pie/cake
les patates	lahs pah-**tah**-tuhs	potatoes
el pebre	uhl **peh**-bruh	pepper
el peix	uhl **pehsh**	fish
el pernil	uhl puhr-**neel**	cured ham
salat serrà	suh-**lat** sehr-**rah**	
el plàtan	uhl **plah**-tun	banana
el pollastre	uhl poo-**lyah**-struh	chicken
la poma	la **poh**-mah	apple
el porc	uhl **pohr**	pork
les postres	lahs **pohs**-truhs	dessert
rostit	rohs-**teet**	roast
la sal	lah **sahl**	salt
la salsa	lah **sahl**-suh	sauce
les salsitxes	lahs sahl-**see**-chuhs	sausages
sec	**sehk**	dry
la sopa	lah **soh**-puh	soup
el sucre	uhl-**soo**-kruh	sugar
la taronja	lah tuh-**rohn**-djuh	orange
el te	uhl teh	tea
les torrades	lahs too-**rah**-thuhs	toast
la vedella	lah veh-**theh**-lyuh	beef
el vi blanc	uhl **bee blang**	white wine
el vi negre	uhl **bee neh**-gruh	red wine
el vi rosat	uhl **bee** roo-**zaht**	rosé wine
el vinagre	uhl bee-**nah**-gruh	vinegar
el xai/el be	uhl **shahee**/uhl beh	lamb
la xocolata	lah shoo-koo-**lah**-tuh	chocolate
el xoriç	uhl shoo-**rees**	red sausage

Numbers

0	zero	**seh**-roo
1	un (masc)	oon
	una (fem)	**oon**-uh
2	dos (masc)	dohs
	dues (fem)	**doo**-uhs
3	tres	trehs
4	quatre	**kwa**-truh
5	cinc	seeng
6	sis	sees
7	set	set
8	vuit	**voo**-eet
9	nou	**noh**-oo
10	deu	**deh**-oo
11	onze	**on**-zuh
12	dotze	**doh**-dzuh
13	tretze	**treh**-dzuh
14	catorze	kah-**tohr**-dzuh
15	quinze	**keen**-zuh
16	setze	**set**-zuh
17	disset	dee-**set**
18	divuit	dee-voo-**eet**
19	dinou	dee-**noh**-oo
20	vint	been
21	vint-i-un	been-tee-**oon**
22	vint-i-dos	been-tee-**dohs**
30	trenta	**tren**-tah
31	trenta-un	tren-**tah** oon
40	quaranta	kwuh-**ran**-tuh
50	cinquanta	seen-**kwahn**-tah
60	seixanta	seh-ee-**shan**-tah
70	setanta	seh-**tan**-tah
80	vuitanta	voo-ee-**tan**-tah
90	noranta	noh-**ran**-tah
100	cent	sen
101	cent un	sent oon
102	cent dos	sen dohs
200	dos-cents (masc)	dohs-**sens**
	dues-centes (fem)	doo-uhs sen-tuhs
300	tres-cents	trehs-**senz**
400	quatre-cents	kwah-truh-**senz**
500	cinc-cents	seeng-senz
600	sis-cents	sees-senz
700	set-cents	set-senz
800	vuit-cents	voo-eet-senz
900	nou-cents	noh-oo-cenz
1,000	mil	meel
1,001	mil un	meel oon

Time

one minute	un minut	oon mee-**noot**
one hour	una hora	oo-nuh **oh**-ruh
half an hour	mitja hora	**mee**-juh **oh**-ruh
Monday	dilluns	dee-**lyoonz**
Tuesday	dimarts	dee-**marts**
Wednesday	dimecres	dee-**meh**-kruhs
Thursday	dijous	dee-**zhoh**-oos
Friday	divendres	dee-**ven**-druhs
Saturday	dissabte	dee-**sab**-tuh
Sunday	diumenge	dee-oo-**men**-juh